Don't Call Me Naomi
-Identifying My True Identity

Tyral Thompson

xulon PRESS

Copyright © 2010 by Tyral Thompson

Don't Call Me Naomi
by Tyral Thompson

Printed in the United States of America

ISBN 9781609572099

All rights reserved solely by the author. The author guarantees all contents are original and do not infringe upon the legal rights of any other person or work. No part of this book may be reproduced in any form without the permission of the author. The views expressed in this book are not necessarily those of the publisher.

Unless otherwise indicated, all Scripture quotations are taken from the HOLY BIBLE, NEW INTERNATIONAL VERSION®. NIV®. Copyright © 1973, 1978, 1984 by the International Bible Society. Used by permission of Zondervan. All rights reserved.

www.xulonpress.com

Acknowledgements

I would like to take this opportunity to say a big thanks to my inspirations. First and foremost, my Lord and Savior Jesus Christ for without him, none of this would have been possible, my parents Charles and Margie Jackson for giving me life, my sisters Toni, Teri, Tori (Tyni) and Tracy, my favorite nieces Temeka (Huggy), Tasha (Taffy), and Lakesha, nephews TJ and Marquis, the best children a mother could have Marvin (Mista), Terricia (Sissy), Marc-Christian, Tiara and the child that God sent me to watch over Anthony (Texas) Townsend.

To my Pastor who gave me carte blanche in every project, pushed me past my limits and helped set me up for success, Willie E. Kilpatrick, Sr. Pastor of the Prince of Peace M. B. Church, to my mentor who walked me through and talked me off the ledge time and time again concerning this project and others, a great man of God, Dr. Erskine A. Jones, Pastor of the Sweetest Church in the world, Sweet Home M. B. Church. Did you think I could forget the greatest friend a girl could have Jacqueline Donaldson, who pushed me, pulled me, prayed for me, cried with me, encouraged me, and even carried me, all of that before I started this project, Tachelle Rhiney-hair and Make up, David Dickerson-Photography, Aeesha Bell and to Mr. Hardy O. Searcy, thank you.

Foreword

We are living in a cynical world with its abstract conversations, lifeless relationships and meaningless pursuits towards non-eternal accumulations. What the world needs is a fresh look at our spiritual walk, our godly commitments, and our own idealist Christian character. This book has dared to go into places where others have feared to even touch. This is a bold venture into the psychic of all Christianity. Tyral has dared others to question the very foundation of faulty thinking with regards to our personal responsibility and our truth walk towards godly responsibility. It is time that we release the old self and embrace a true commitment and love for the things of God. This is truly a must read for every believer who has become dreadfully tired of the same "hum ho" lifestyle of the self-righteous and fabulous. This book challenges the status quo of church folk and challenges another level of analytical thinking.

Read this book and prepare yourself for change, it's going to happen. It happened to me! She has woven both her life experiences and the sacredness of scripture in an incredible union of love. The story of Naomi told through the eyes of Tyral are refreshing, renewing, reinforcing and reinventing. I love this book, I absolutely love this book. Hear the spirit of God teach you, motivate you, inspire you and move you.

Believe me you are going on a spiritual journey that will bring you a fresh anointed revelation for your life. Enjoy!

Willie E. Kilpatrick

Table of Contents

Introduction xi

CHAPTER 1

Identity Crisis 17
Loss of Identity 19
ID Tags 21
Dealing with Identity 24
That's Just How I Am 25
Transitional Tools 27
- Reflect 27
- React 29
- Reveal 31

CHAPTER 2

Position 34
How Did I Get Here 34
Training 36
Under Construction 38
Deconstruction 41
- Widow 43
- Single 45
- Married 48

CHAPTER 3
Conversion 52
Harvest Time 52
Stages 54
- Denial - Deal 55-57
- Anger - Allowance 58-59
- Bargaining - Beginning 60-61
- Depression - Deliverance 62-63
- Acceptance - Anticipation 64

Picking up the Pieces 65
It Just So Happened 66

CHAPTER 4
Character Concerns 69
Knowing His Role 71
Security 72
- Physical Protection 73
- Personality Protection 75
- Provisional Protection 77

Proper Placement 79

CHAPTER 5
It's all Relative 81
Am I What I Want 81
Qualities and Attributes 83
Clean Up 85
Selfless Sacrifice 87
- Redemption 89
- Love 92

Conclusion 92

Introduction

Sitting in a mostly empty classroom of a local high school, I found myself in a workshop that I was attending to gain credits related to the ministry I was choosing to work in, within my church. Newly widowed and newly accepting of my call to ministry, "just go, learn what you can learn and get what you can get," was my attitude. Sitting in the front of the classroom was a very astute looking woman, seemingly middle aged with a calm and peaceful demeanor about herself. She began a dissertation about the Book of Ruth and how it compared to her life. She talked about how she had lost her husband and all of the different emotions she and her children had gone through. Personally, I didn't want to hear that, I was going through the same thing. I had lost my husband, I had young children and I was a widow as well. What made her story so great that she could teach a class? Oh she was a Pastors wife, she was a mother, she lost her husband, recovered and she was a teacher. Well, I guess she put her time in. So I sat and I listened. The class lasted a couple of days. She gave instruction and she gave home work assignments. After the first day, I still wasn't speaking much in class. I really didn't want to tell my story, but seemingly, everyone else did. So one by one, of the five or six of us that were in there, they began to share. By the last day of class, I could actually see what it was that this instructor, this lady, this formative, well put together woman of God was trying to get us to see. I lowered my guard and I began to share.

From this initial workshop, I began to study the Book of Ruth (on my own) and became very familiar with the struggles of these two women and how the lives they were living and the issues they were dealing with were some of the same ones that I had. If I was dealing with these same struggles, I knew some other women were also.

As I began to read, study and understand this small book, I began to identify with the two main characters of the story. At first I identified mainly with Naomi. She is the first to be introduced as a woman that seems to basically have it all. She has a husband, a home in a beautiful land and children, sons to be exact, which held a higher status than just being married or having daughters. Their family must soon leave the home they had and move to unfamiliar territory. A territory filled with things opposite of what they know, filled with things different than they have been brought up with and filled with certain things that they have possibly only heard about. After leaving their home, some hurtful things begin to happen to Naomi which ends up leaving her angry at the Lord and bitter about her life. As I watch Naomi go through this story I realize that she transitions from one area in life to another; sometimes a little bit smoother than others. It seems as though Naomi loses her identity when she looses her place, her position and her provisions. Naomi loses her place when she is moved from her home land to a foreign land. She loses her position when her husband dies and she is transformed from a wife to a widow. Lastly, she loses her provisions when her sons die and she has no one to care for her. She is no longer feeling like who she is or what her name describes, but she is putting on the label of her situation and her circumstances and what they describe.

Within the story of Naomi's transitions, we meet Ruth who is also transitioning into and out of some unknown areas of her life. I can also identify with her. She has also lost a loved one, leaving her family and home land, gaining new knowledge and a new found friendship through loyalty. We also meet a man named Boaz, whose name means "in him is strength," who shows his support of these two women through protection and provisions.

As women, situations and circumstances have left us feeling less than who we are. Things have occurred in our lives that leave us questioning our true identities; as wives, how we identify as daughters, how we feel we should identify as mothers, and the multiple identities as sisters and friends. We question our own self-image, how we are measuring up to the idealisms of others, and the multiple positions that we have been placed in. Through it all we try to transition from one area of our lives to another. At times we get stuck in what seems most comfortable or even what is most critical because we cannot seem to move. Transition is not an easy task. There are steps that must be taken to do it. You cannot expect to go from one place to another by sitting still. Some transitions will be smooth and some will take a lot of effort on your part. There is someplace to begin and at some point, there will be an ending.

Through the many transitions Naomi and Ruth encounter, they will find that transition through relocation brings duty by dedication. Ruth will show her dedication to Naomi by pledging to go with her, stay with her, live with her, and die with her. There will be times in your life that you must move from one place to the next. Relocation sometimes is the best way to transition. There will be times in your life that you must move from one place to the next, but you must know when it's the best time to relocate. At times we move when it is right, and at times we move too fast. Relocation is more than physically packing up your belongings and going someplace else. It may have to start with changing your mindset from one thought process to another. You may have to move away from a relationship. You may have to leave one job to take another or you may have to remove yourself from one situation or circumstance to get into another position. Changing your way of thinking may help begin the transitional process of relocation. You will know its time to relocate when where you are is not nourishing you anymore. When you are no longer being sustained in this area, in this place, in this relationship, it is then time to move on, time to relocate. Naomi left at the urging of her husband because the land was lacking. There was no more food in the land and conditions were no longer sustaining their needs, so they relocated to another land. Within Naomi's transition, she moved to the place that she originally relocated from for the same reason she initially left. She left the place because it was lacking and she returned to the same place she left because, it too was lacking. There was not enough to sustain her, not enough to keep her there. Often times we find ourselves returning to familiar situations or circumstances for the same reason we left; not enough love, affection or attention to sustain us or not enough money to keep us there. We may initially leave our parents home for want of independence and find ourselves returning home so that we may regain our independence.

At times when you move, you must be dedicated to the move so that you may be delivered from the position which you are in. Dedication takes every effort and commitment that you feel deep within yourself. Dedication takes a strong understanding of leaving what is behind you to move forward to what will be your future. This is also a story of revelation; revelation that you can be more than you actually thought you were. Although you wear many jackets some of the ones you wear identify you more than the others. This is a story of commitment; commitment of being connected by a common cause. The women must share by connecting with one another and showing concern for the care of one another.

These two women find themselves in similar situations. In this book you will find ways to connect with other women. You will be reminded of connections you have made or that you would like to make with others. You will notice the care these women have and the concern that you share with others. During their transitions from one area of their lives to another, the final things the women find is restoration; restoration of faith and restoration of hope through the works and the acts that they will perform. Respecting one another and refreshing one another until the final act of redemption is made through the selfless acts of Boaz to renew the lives of these two women. Restoration comes with faith; faith that you can do anything that you set out to do, and faith that you can be whatever it is and whoever it is that you choose to be. Restoration comes through respect; respect for your body, your mind and your sense of being. The respect of others for your time, your space and your truths, and respect for the same concerning others and those around you. Please read the book of Ruth before you read this book or even along side it. Reading this book hopefully help you transition from the areas of your life that you are finding more difficult to maneuver alone.

CHAPTER 1   Identity Crisis

Growing up in the seventies and eighties, I was the youngest of five girls. I'm sure by the time I had come along, my parents figured same thing, different child. Having another girl was nothing new and nothing special. I was not treated badly by any means, I was still the baby of the family. I felt as though there was no originality in my upbringing. I found myself in constant shadows and consistent groups within the family. I was always known as one of the Jackson girls and to some of my relatives I was known as "Number five". By the time I entered elementary school early, I found myself in the same grade as my older sister where some people thought of us as twins. There were things that we shared; things that were considered ours. Our friends, our room, our clothes. To me, it really didn't matter, I accepted whatever, I wore whatever and I did whatever would keep the peace. Hand me downs were just fine as long as they covered me up. I was far from popular. I was thin, very slender, tall and flat in all the wrong places. In these times that would be great, but in the seventies and eighties, curves were in. I didn't really take much thought to my appearance because I thought, "Who sees me anyway?" I was experiencing an identity crisis. The real me was being covered up by layers.

At some point I realized our friends were really her friends, they were really not there for me. I soon began to develop my own friends and when I say develop, I mean make up. There was one personality I adopted that was the hard mean girl that talked about people and would start fights. Never really had to fight on her own, but she would start plenty. This was a way to alienate myself from rest of the crowd. Then there was my favorite, I call her Joanna Banana. She was a jokester, very funny and a fun loving girl who loved to make people laugh. She didn't worry about what people said about her or what they thought of her. She would make fun of herself in attempt to shield herself from the pains of it coming from others. She would come out more often than the next, but those two personas carried me all the way through high school. I remember my Senior Memories book where people were supposed to write all kinds of nice things about you. One thing in particular that was written by my mother stood out. It said something to the effect of you cannot always hide behind a clowns face. I'm sure it had more, but that is what I vividly remember because it was when I realized my attempt to hide my true self. To me, she was saying that I could not continue to hide my emotions and feelings behind a false personality, and to deal with my issues *as* myself. To me, my issues were more easily dealt with if I didn't deal with them. So I let her, Joanna Banana, deal with them. It seemed that every year after that, I decided as my new years resolution, I would stop being a clown, I would stop acting up and I would let the real me come out. In all actuality, as long as I had acted this way, she was who I had become and that was how I was known. It was easier to feel this way than to accept what was really going on in my life. I felt the real me had been taken over, but there was a battle going on inside for the real me to be free. Would I continue to fight for freedom or would I just give up and let her (Joanna Banana) be the real me? My identity was in crisis.

Loss of Identity

Shortly out of high school, I met and married my first husband. He was only a year older than me, but he had an "old spirit." My husband was one of the youngest members of a gospel quartet group. The older members all had wives and children with some of the children close to our age. These were the men he looked up to. He attempted to emulate them and took their advice concerning our marriage. My greeting from most of these older men would be calling me by my title as wife and my husband's first name. I'm not sure if any of them knew my first name. I was either "Mrs. Marvin" or "his wife." My husband would soon carry on this tradition. There were things like this which was just things that were expected of me to accept because I was "his wife." I was losing my identity more and more.

Over the years a lot of things accumulate and build up within us. Let's call these things layers. The reason for calling them layers is because some of them we have used to cover us up and we carry them around upon our backs. Some of these layers have weighed us down and in turn buried the real person underneath. We have covered up the struggles and the stigmas we have gone through. We have dressed up family secrets, covered years of abuse with make-up and fed our discontentment's with food. All the while, thinking that if we just make ourselves busy enough, throw ourselves into work and family activities, we won't have to worry about it. Constantly adding more layers. We watch TV, movies, videos and soap operas in an attempt to attach these identities on top of the layers we already have because we still don't know who we are. This is where we begin to lose our identity in an attempt to become someone else. Hair like Halle Berry, house like Jill Abbott, closets like Kimora Lee, and carrying around so much stuff with other peoples names on it you look like a walking billboard. You don't want to be like you, so you strive to be like her. Who are you really? Do you know? You know who you think you are, but what you are doing is ultimately chasing who you think you want to be. Attempting to live through your children by making them out to be the ultimate cheerleader that you always wanted to be or the ball player that you thought you were, the ballerina that gets all the attention, or the musician that you could have been. Putting them in activity after activity, class after class, play after play. You are now stealing their identities from them.

Until you begin to remove the layers of stigma of what people have called you, until you remove the layers of what people said you could never accomplish, until you remove the layers of doubt and discontentment, you will never know who you are. In turn, you will never be all that God intended for you to be. You have lost your true identity underneath all of the words, phrases, acts and spirits that you have allowed to cover you.

One day you look back and you begin to question, is this really who I am? Am I really that mean? Am I really that fast? Am I really that bossy? Am I really that quiet? You have been covered by all of these layers so long, that you don't know how to come from underneath them. Some of them have caused so much pain, that you don't even want to come from underneath them. It's considered comfortable, stable, and you are content. Its all you know.

You don't have to stay in that place, you don't have to stay covered up by all of those things. Begin to remove the layers one at a time. Don't overwhelm yourself by trying to take off everything at one time. You may not be able to handle it. Start at the top layer and figure out what has you bogged down right now. What is causing you the current pain, and reoccurring stress? Remove that first. When you get that layer off, lay it to the side, take a break and work on the next thing. Be mindful of what you are removing so that you don't leave yourself too vulnerable.

ID Tags

"Don't call me Naomi," she told them. "Call me Mara"
Ruth 1:20a

Naomi was facing things in her life that caused her not to feel like who she really was, and she was attempting to take on another persona. So I wondered, why in the world would she not want to be called by her name? Her name meant *Pleasant*. Why would she not want to be called *Pleasant*? Because her condition was bitter, her situation was bitter. It caused her to feel bitter and she personally tagged her identity by her present emotion. Naomi had been married, she had two sons and she had come from a place that was the Promised Land given to the children of Israel by God. A "land of bread" by name, Bethlehem Judah. By any means of the word, Naomi was at one time considered blessed. At the time she makes this statement, Naomi had moved her family to Moab, a lace of idol worshipers and false gods. She has lost her husband and her status as a married woman.

Her sons have married women from this land and now brought them into the home along with her. As she relied on her sons now for her care, they too have succumbed to death. Naomi now returns to her home land only to be partially recognized by the women that she once walked beside, worked beside and lived beside. But she is not the wealthy, distinguished woman, wife and mother that she once was. Naomi is now poor, childless and widowed and she feels very bitter. The circumstances and situations that Naomi has been through in her past causes her to feel bitter, and she no longer associates with her identity. Naomi once identified with her titles of mother and wife, when those titles were taken away; she felt as if she was no longer who she was born to be. Naomi didn't realize what her destiny was, what God had for her.

We connect freely to certain titles such as wife, mother or sister but we don't understand the total significance of what it means or who we are supposed to be within that title. Have you ever just not felt like being a wife? You have made the commitment to the title, and you are dedicated to the role, but wonder if that is your destiny? You wake up one day and you are thinking, "is this really all I'm going to be?" Some days you just don't feel like a mother. You are in the store with your children, stressed and on the phone or otherwise occupied by the magazines displayed in the grocery line, and in the background you hear little junior call your name for the fifteenth time. "Mamma!", and you say, "Don't call me Mamma, I'm changing my name!" Now technically, you know that you cannot change your name. They could call you anything you could make up, Nana, Miss Lady or Mother. But when you are in a position of discontentment or bitterness for the position, it doesn't matter what they call you, you just don't want them to call you at all. Some women have even connected to a tag that has a negative connotation no matter how you look at it. Some say it describes the certain strength in a woman, or a particular type of attitude. I say if you are a woman of God, it should not describe you at all. You should not accept being called *it*, nor should you call anyone by *it* and you certainly should not identify yourself as *it*. If you want to describe yourself as a strong woman, describe yourself as virtuous.

Naomi wanted to disconnect from her name, but she didn't realize that her name was her destiny. Her feeling was bitter, but her future was pleasant. Occasionally things will occur that we have no understanding as to why God would allow it. Why would he allow my children to die, my husband to die, my divorce, and so much pain? Why would he allow all those bad things to happen to me? Because we don't understand the reason, we blame him. It may not seem at the time that the things you are going through are for your good. You may think that is the worst thing that could ever happen to you or that you are the only one that has ever been through it. Sometimes bad things happen to good people. It may have been by no fault of your own or nothing you had done, but God knows what you can handle. You are a vessel of greatness that God has utilized for his works. Some things he had to let you go through so that there would be a path to what he is bringing you to. God does not want us to walk through life being victims to one thing or another, going day by day letting life happen. God is perfecting you for your purpose so that you can help someone else. When there is a tag of identification, an ID tag, it gives you information about the product that is inside the package. God has tagged you as great and he has identified you as precious. Check your ID tag and see what's on it.

We have done things, gone through things, felt things, and things have hurt us. Do you think because you change your name, you will change the things about you? No, your destiny is connected to who you are. God knows who you are and he has a plan for you. Changing your name is not going to change who you are or whose you are. To be who God intends for you to be, you must change your inside. Changing will take work, time and dedication. You can read one hundred self help books, hear one thousand sermonic messages on change or receive one million encouraging words from friends and family, but if you never personally, physically, emotionally and spiritually do things to change your circumstance or situation, it will never change. You must deal with your past to change your future.

Dealing with Identity

It would take many years and many broken resolutions to finally come to who I really am and to be comfortable with that person. There are so many of us today that are suffering the same identity crisis as Naomi. We have no idea who we really are or who we are supposed to be.

We have tried on different personalities and titles in hopes that one would fit like a good pair of your favorite shoes. But we soon find that they are either too big, too small, too tight or too high. We can't walk in them or they just make our feet hurt more. Just like a well made pair of shoes, each are intended for specific purposes and you must be able to transition into them. The transition must be smooth and done with ease. You cannot go from always wearing flats to walking in four inch heals. You have to transition into them. You may have to walk around the house in them, going up and down the stairs, carrying weight in them and then deal with the discomforts as they come. Same goes with the titles and the roles we find ourselves in. You have to learn to transition into them before you can walk comfortably in them and deal with the discomforts as they come.

To be able to deal with your identity you must know what forms your personality. Everything you've touched, witnessed, and experienced from a child, aware that you were in the world, has formed you into the person that you are today. People you have been in contact with, places you have lived, places you have visited, if you moved a lot, if you had both parents at home, if you were raised by your grandmother, if you were rich or if you considered yourself poor, the position you held in the family unit, if you were the first born, the middle child or the baby of the family, all of these things combined and more have formed you into the person you are. There are certain instances that we can all share with same generation persons. Some of the same things you were accustomed to, so was the next person. By the same token, some things you've experienced, I have never had the privilege. These things help you make the decisions that you make once you become an adult. These things help you decide where you will live, who you will date or marry, how many children you want, if you will attend a higher education institution, and even what kind of profession you would choose. These things make you react a certain way to a certain situation, some of which will get a great reaction from one, will get no reaction from another.

If you push these things aside and act like they never occurred in your life, you will find yourself hiding from yourself. Some of us would like to change our past. Some of the things we saw, felt or lived, we would just like to forget about. I wish it were that easy, but its not. You cannot forget about your past, but you can get past it. You first have to acknowledge it. If you don't deal with your past, it will deal with you.

That's just how I am

We have all heard this statement. "That's just how I am" or, "That's just how she is." To me, and this is just to me, this statement is a cop out. This statement is usually made about someone who is seemingly out of control and no one wants to approach them to attempt to get them to change. This person is usually accepting of the fact that they are hard to get along with and the people around them also accept this and use it as an excuse not to deal with them so they consider themselves loners. They possibly feel as though life has dealt them a hard blow, they are bitter and angry and this is just how they are going to be for the rest of their lives. They may be loud, they may be easily angered, feel a sense of entitlement, or even slip into depression with any bad news. Afflictions can make you bitter and loss can make you sorrowful but I cannot believe that anyone chooses to be unhappy, mean or unbearable. But because of the situations and circumstances that occurred in their lives, those shoes may hurt. Instead of taking them off, they keep wearing them, keep walking, and keep being hurt. It has been my experience when dealing with these people that they make some attempts to be accepted and to be loved. Occasionally, they try to reach out, but pretty soon they slip back into what is considered their comfort zone. I'm almost positive that the place they are is not all that comfortable. We live in the shadows of what others think of us. We are very conscious of what is being said about us and we have developed tough skin so that we can deal. Instead of becoming a mirror and reflecting what is shown to us, we become a wall so that things can effectively bounce off of us. People will definitely have an opinion about you, regardless of how you behave or how you are, but you must realize it's not what you are called that defines you, it's what you answer to. You cannot allow other peoples perception of you to define you. At some point in our lives we must get to a place that we no longer blame God or others for the way we are today. You must find a place in your life where you no longer blame your father for not being there as the reason you need a man in your life. You no longer say because she didn't love me the way I needed, I don't need love, because I was treated different, I am different. These are excuses for not being all that you can be. Reasons are able to stand, excuses fall away. As I asked a group of women what the difference between reasons and excuses were, four out of five said there was no difference. Their thinking is that reasons are just justified excuses for getting away with bad behavior. But understand that there is a difference. Using this analogy for instance: Turn signals are placed on the front and rear of each vehicle to let the people in front of you and/or the people behind you know which direction you intend to turn (reason); the different justifications we utilize for not using the turn signals time and time again, are excuses. Yes some things happened and that thing caused you to be a certain way, but do you have to stay that way? No, you don't have to stay that way. There is a way out, and that way out is through transition. You may find that people want to change; they just don't have the tools necessary to change. There are certain things that you must recognize if you want to transition from the hurt, pain and despair to a life of love, peace and prosperity. I want to give you the tools I believe will help you to transition.

TRANSITIONIAL TOOLS

Transition is described as a move from one position, place or stage to another. Transition is a process, and it probably won't occur over night. Transition takes time and effort.

Naomi recognized that some things in her life had gone terribly wrong. By moving from her land of promise and through death and loss, she realized that some things had occurred that caused change in her circumstances. Not everything you do will cause change. Sometimes change will occur through no fault or action of your own, but when change does occur, you may find yourself at a loss of what to do. A tool is just a device that will aid you in performing specific tasks or duties. Having the proper tools and knowing which ones to use at the right time in the right sequence will help make the transition easier. Here are a few tools you can use to help you through transitions. Utilizing these transitional tools will assist you in moving from one area to the next. The first thing you must do is reflect.

Reflect: When you reflect, you take a little time to calmly and reasonably think about a certain situation that has already occurred, taking into account all of the information and considering the realization of it. Now, some of us may have to go back a little bit further than others when we do our reflection to realize the initial moment the event took place. Often times we don't really want to think about it, it may cause too much pain or take you back to the feelings you felt at the time. Instead of reflecting, we start suppressing; holding things in, covering things up or refusing to acknowledge anything happened at all. Not thinking about it, doesn't remove it from your mind or from your experiences. Memories are not supposed to go away, that's why they are called memories. Reflecting often causes one certain emotion that we are sometimes afraid to express; tears. Why is it that we are afraid to cry? One of the biggest reasons I hear for not wanting to look back on things is because "it will make me cry." Why have we adopted such a negative idealism to such a human action? Many emotions can cause a woman to cry including fear, excitement, joy, pain, happiness and even anguish. I believe that tears are a way of a temporary release.

My mother often uses this saying "you pay for your raising." Generally she uses it when my children are doing something that makes me shake my head in shame, and she is saying that these are some of the actions that I did when I was a child, so the fact that my children are doing it and it looks ten times worse, is just the principle of reaping and sowing being put into practice. The things I have scattered in their lives, a little bit planted here and a little bit there, has grown and multiplied and they are now giving it back to me pressed down, shaken together and running over. When I think of that statement "you pay for your raising" I think that everything that I experienced growing up, whether good or bad, affected me in some way. The different things that have been scattered about here and there, planted in me and covered up, grew and multiplied and now I have to compensate for it in some way. I may pay with my health, or with my

Don't Call Me Naomi

emotions. I may even pay with my actions, but I will in some way give something of myself for what it is that I received, took in, and allowed to grow. If you never reflect on certain aspects of what happened in your life and what is occurring from the way you look at things, you may never be able to transition into the next place in your life. You will be stuck in your present reality, or your past, possibly believing that nothing ever changes.

If you are trying to help someone transition or you are doing so yourself, you may have to point out certain truths to help reflect on the past experiences. Naomi's truth was that her husband moved them away from their home, took them away from a land of promise to a land of perversions, and then he died. Naomi's truth was that all that she had was gone, her husband, her sons, her reputation, and her resources. Naomi's truth was that she was angry, and bitter. Your truth is whatever happened to you in your past that has you angry, hurt and possibly even bitter. Those things that are keeping you stuck justifying your actions and your feelings time after time. Your truth may be rape, your truth may be debt, your truth may be loss, or your truth may be that you had a child at a young age but you must reflect on that and move from it. Think clearly about what happened, consider all of the avenues surrounding it and realize what is really true about it. You may find that it was not your fault, you were not to blame, you are worthy of love, and you don't have to stay bound by it because you can move on. Naomi didn't stay in that land where all of her pain occurred. Your predicament or position does not have to be permanent.

React: Once you have begun to reflect on your past and some things begin to come into light, you may wonder, what do I do now? Now that I'm broke, what do I do now, now that I have cancer? What do I do now, now that he left? What do I do now? Now you must react. Reaction is a change in response to something that causes stimulation. Your reflection and what you discover from it, should have caused some sort of stimulation. Reaction is what you do now after this thing has happened to you to transform your thoughts or actions. How you react to your reflection is determined by your mindset. Some people will react by lashing out at others. We are hurting so we want to make others feel the pain we feel. Some of us react by acting out. We want everyone to know that something happened but we can't express it, so we express it in ways of addiction or attitude and some react by not reacting at all. Now is the time in the midst of the transition that you begin to show some sort of change. How you reacted to situations and circumstances before, cannot be how you react now. One of the ways to react is to first acknowledge what is your present reality. Naomi gains information relevant to her future. Yes her husband is dead, yes her sons are gone also, yes she is left with the pain and the loss, but while she is still in the place of her pain, she hears that the place of her promise was again a place of provisions, so she made preparation to return there. That was her reaction to her reflection. What will your reaction be to your reflection? No I didn't do all that I could do, Yes some of the blame was mine, and once you look back and come to a realization, your next move should be to gain information to help you move on. Develop a way to get closer to the next step in your transition. One good move would be forgiveness. Begin to drop some stuff off at your spiritual garage. Your spiritual garage is where you place all of your hurts, your fears, your discontentment and pains. You store them up until you can go back, find the proper place for them to either be disposed or distributed. Distribution may come in during revelation, so let's concentrate on the disposal here. *1 Peter 5:7 says Cast all your anxiety on him because he cares for you.* Give it all to God, when you lay it upon the alter, leave it there for him to take care of it.

God offers forgiveness for us if we ask him for it. Gaining forgiveness from others sometimes is not so easy. Once you place something in your spiritual garage and are granted the Grace of forgiveness by God, never allow anyone else to get it out and bring it back to you. Begin to work on forgiveness. Forgiveness through prayer. One thing I love about God's forgiving quality is that he asks first that you are forgiving. *And when you stand praying, if you hold anything against any, forgive him, so that your Father in heaven may forgive your sins. Mark 11:25.* The first person you should forgive is yourself if you played any part in it. Forgiveness is not acting like everything is ok or saying that nothing happened. When you forgive, you are just saying I won't hold this against you any more. You are granting a pardon for the occurrence. I don't have to be your best friend, I don't have to share a meal with you, but I won't hold this event against you anymore because it is holding me down. You may find it difficult at first to forgive, but forgiveness comes when it is given. So my mode of thinking is "How dare Me with my sinful self, refuse to forgive someone for something they have said or done to me?" I have knowingly and unknowingly done or said things to others to hurt or harm them. I am responsible for my actions and my reactions. How I react helps me move to a different level because I'm not holding onto things on this level. Prayer helps take you to another level.

Reveal: *Forget the former things; do not dwell in the past. See, I am doing a new thing! Now it springs up; do you not perceive it? I am making a way in the desert and streams in the wasteland. Isaiah 43:18-19*

What a revelation! Has the voice of God ever told you he was going to do a new thing in your life? You have asked for change and prayed for a new existence because you were tired of doing things the same way. God has heard your prayers and he is already answering them. You just don't see him at work just yet. Although you may not see the plan that He has for you, know that there is a plan. God wants you to be happy, and he wants you to live a peaceful existence. Revealing is making known what is hidden. When God reveals things to you, you must be in a position to notice what he has done. We ask God to show us with signs and we sometimes even ask him to allow us to see things about ourselves and others. When he shows us, we must be willing to see what he has. Should your mind be crowded with negative thoughts and your vision clouded by sights from your past, you will not be able to see the new things he has in store for you. You must open your mind to new thoughts, new ideas and new visions to be able to see what it is God is trying to show you.

Naomi was returning home, to people she knew, but she was coming from a land of idol worshipers and a land where they served pagan gods. When she started off, her daughters-in-law were with her, at some point in their travels, Naomi decides to send them back to their families. She had been with these women in their land for over ten years, why would she not want them to go back to her land with her? Maybe she didn't want anyone to know how she had been living. She had been living without a husband, without sons, without proper support, in idolatrous land with idolatrous women. Maybe she didn't want to bring a reminder of her past with her. Maybe you don't want anyone to know what happened to you, how you were feeling, how you were treated or how you once lived. The very thing you are trying to hide may be the very thing that God wants to use to help you go further. When you reveal that thing that has kept you in the dark, when you reveal that thing that has kept you down, when you bring forth those issues that were keeping you in bondage, no one else can hold them over your head and no one else can use them against you. You release the

Don't Call Me Naomi

power of shame and you may find that those are the very things you can use to help someone else. Initially, Naomi didn't realize that she was meant to be more than just a wife and mother. That was only the basis that God set as a foundation. Before she could help Ruth deal with the changes in her life, God laid the groundwork for Naomi to transition through her own changes. She had to find a way to deal with what she had been through so she could help others. Naomi had left her home town, she could understand Ruth leaving hers. Naomi had to go thru her loss so she could be a vessel for Ruth. Look at the groundwork God has laid in your life. You are meant for more; you *are* the head and not the tail, you *are* worthy of love, you *are* a good parent, you *are* smart enough, you *are* important enough, and people *do* care about you. The sooner you recognize that, the sooner you will be able to reveal it to others.

Chapter 2 Position

How did I get here?

A recent conversation with one of my friends revealed to me one surprising fact about my life. I have never been alone. In all my life, I have never lived alone. I have always lived in a home with someone else. I grew up in the home with my mother and my sisters. Over the years they began to grow up and move out. I was still there with my mother and another sister. I graduated high school and moved away, but I moved in with my oldest sister. When another sister also decided to move, we got a place together. I then married my first husband and began to have children. So, I have always been in a home with someone else; parents, siblings, husbands or children. I have never been alone.

As I transitioned from child, to adult, single to married, and wife to mother, sometimes my transition was not that smooth. When I was born, I was automatically a sister, didn't have to do anything and I didn't have to have any skills. It was automatic. I just was a sister. This was my position. So as I grew up, always being a part of someone else's life. I just thought this was automatically my position, what I'm supposed to do, who I'm supposed to be.

When you were born a little girl, I'm sure you were the most beautiful thing that your mother and father had ever seen. You were probably dressed in pink, and as a small child allowed to play with baby dolls and doll houses, kitchen sets and dress up clothes. You may have played house, dreamed of your wedding day, decided how many kids you wanted and what you wanted to be when you grew up. Eventually you transition into a young lady and you dreamt of being a wife and mother, having your own home or starting a career. BUT WHAT HAPPENED? When you look at your life right now, is it everything you dreamed? Anything you hoped? At all what you imagined? Why? Maybe the position you are in is not the position for you right now. It is hard to transition into a position and work well in that position if you know nothing about the position. Have you ever taken a job that you thought you were qualified for, only to start work and realize that you are lost and it is a lot harder to do than you thought?

Some of us went from daughter to wife, some went from daughter to mother, some of us were sisters to sisters, some of us sisters to brothers, some of us became aunts before we knew what it was to be a niece. Some of us have gone from single to married, and back to single again. Some from married to widowed before we got a hang of being married, just out of being single. Lastly some of us were forced or thrown into positions of maturity that our minds and bodies were not ready for maybe having to raise younger siblings or even from being abused. You have a few options on figuring out if you are in the right position or if you are where you are supposed to be. You can either quit, keep working lost and confused, or you can ask someone for help.

Sometimes we think that things are just automatic, and because we are women, we should just know. Some things in life are automatic, natural behaviors. No one has to show you how to do it. But there are a few things in life, you have to learn. You must learn to be a wife, you must learn to be a mother, and you must even learn to be single. There must be some type of training in each of these positions so that you can operate efficiently in each. Some of these positions you may never hold in your lifetime. You may choose to never be a mother and you may choose to never be a wife but if you do choose to do so, get proper training. You can't just assume a position and expect to know everything about it if you haven't had proper training. When you gain the training, it is just as important that you utilize the information gained for it to work. Just knowing it is not enough. For instance, say you are trained to use a parachute. Sitting through the classes and taking notes is not enough. When the time comes for you to jump from the plane and you don't pull the cord, you have just wasted your time and you hit the ground hard. Put into practice the information that you gain, so that when you need it, you know how to use it. Don't say I will wait until I get married to learn how to be a wife. I'll wait until I have a baby to learn to be a mother. Get the information, practice your craft by being good to yourself. Keep your own house clean, cook meals for yourself, help take care of your siblings, your relatives, work in the church. Practice until it is your season to walk in your position.

Training

When you were growing up, If you played with dolls, washing their hair, giving them baths, and dressing them, that is an informal mode of training, but training none the less. If you were taught to clean your room, make a meal, wash dishes and do laundry, if you baby sat every now and then, that was training. It is not automatic for you to just know how to cook because you are a woman. Some young girls stood in the kitchen with their mothers and grandmothers, watched and learned the proper techniques, picked up on the recipes and developed knowledge for cooking. Some young girls were done a disservice by their parents without thought of it being such. They just wanted to give them a better life so they were never made or shown how to do much of anything. If you grew up and you never had to make your bed, you never had chores, you never set the table for the family dinner, your clothes were always set out for you, your laundry was always folded neatly in your drawers, the meals were just sitting at the table when you arrived and everything was always done for you, don't be surprised if you wake up one day in your own place and it looks like a natural disaster. You must be trained and learn the behavior needed to be a woman, learn to be a mother, a wife, a good friend. Good training takes dedication, and dedication takes a lot of time and energy. You cannot be dedicated to too many things at one time. I know we have all become "superwoman" taking on many tasks at one time. We are mother, wife, executive, confidant and sister. We have taken on multiple roles in the home such as cook, maid, partner, bill payer, doctor, nurse, and counselor. We have taken on roles at work such as, partner, copier, secretary, leader, CEO, HNIC, managing departments, cohorts and such. We even take on multiple roles in the church such as, ministers, leaders, directors, councils, task assistants, fellowships, committees and in all of this, you say you are dedicated. Wrong, you cannot multitask in dedication. This is where we go wrong, we think we can handle it, we can do it and we have it all under control, but in reality, it has us under control. That is where I believe the phrase, "Jack of all trades, master of none," comes from. We try to do it all, but before we know it, we are worn out, torn down, and completely drained of all our energy and when we look back on what was actually accomplished, something suffered. You cannot be effective if you are dedicated to too many things at one time. Yes, you can multitask. You can focus on more than one thing at a time, but just know that something is going to lack. You cannot be 100% effective at home and be 100% effective at church, while still holding down a full time job while trying to becoming a full time student. It just doesn't work like that. Begin to remove the layers of your life by eliminating tasks, jobs, duties and assignments one at a time. Make a list of your priorities and start at the top. Figure out what is most important and vital to your survival at this particular time, and begin there. You cannot do it all, in reality, you are not supposed to. Train someone else to fill your position in certain areas, so that you will be free to concentrate on the priorities in your life. Overextending yourself is not healthy for your mind or body. Train your daughters to write checks and pay bills. Train your sons to cook and do laundry. It will free up some of your time while teaching them skills needed for adult life. *Train up a child in the way that he should go: and when he is old he will not depart from it. Proverbs 22:6 (KJV)* Take that time and dedicate it to you and God for restoration.

Under Construction

Construction areas pop up here and there, on our highways, in our neighborhoods, industrial areas and on basic city streets. There are boundaries set up right outside the construction area that may read Construction Zone or Area Under Construction. Either way, this is to inform you that there is work being done in this area. You may go into a construction area and never see any work being done, but if you pass by there enough times, there will be progress made. Eventually you will begin to see the project taking shape. When you are building character, people may just see all of the jumbled pieces of material, and not see all of the work being done behind the scenes. There used to be a time when older women wouldn't mind telling younger women what was right. And there was a time that younger women respected what older women had to say. *Titus 2:4-5 says Then they can train the younger women to love their husbands and children, to be self controlled and pure, to be busy at home, to be kind and to be subject to their husbands, so that no one will malign the word of God.* Older women didn't mind telling younger women, keep yourself pure, respect your elders, respect yourself. They would tell you how to dress appropriately for any occasion, how to keep a clean house, how to manage a home, and say "yes ma'am" and "no ma'am." With the changing of the times, instead of the older women telling you what is right, they refuse to say anything because the younger women are not always accepting. I have heard women say, that they could not tell me anything because they had done it themselves, but I believe that there are some holes I should not have to fall into. Maybe I should not have so many relationship issues. Maybe I should have an easier time raising my kids. Maybe there is another way to deal with the father of my children. There are things that some women have done or some things that they have gone through that were dangerous and devastating that construction signs would have been helpful. Warning, don't go down this road, danger ahead! Relationships we have tried, people we have run into or positions that have been taken. I know you may have done it, but tell me how it turned out so that I don't have to go down that same road if the choice arises. There is nothing new under the sun, so don't believe that you are the only one dealing with a particular situation. The situation may be new to you, but it is not new. If no one wants to tell of how they got over or how they got out then young women will continue to make the same mistakes over and over again. There is no reason to allow someone to make their own mistakes or for anyone to want to make their own mistakes. You will never know it all, but what you do know, you should share. Someone will be rewarded for their obedience. Naomi and Ruth shared. This was Naomi's homeland, it was all new to Ruth. She had to be willing to listen to what Naomi had to tell her. She was respectful of the information she received. I'm sure the journey from Moab to

Bethlehem was full of information that was going to be vital to the survival of both women. At this point, they needed each other to survive. Ruth had to trust Naomi's wisdom, Naomi had to trust Ruth's willingness. Ruth's willingness to listen to the wisdom of Naomi resulted in a new transition for her. Ruth being the younger of the two women finds herself in the same position as Naomi. They have both lost their husbands and are now widowed. Naomi is attempting to understand her new role. She was a wife and mother, now she is single, childless and a widow. Naomi questions if she could have more sons, and states that she had hope that she could have another husband, would that in fact change her present status. Ruth also had to identify with her identity and by doing that, she realizes that the life she had before, she no longer wanted. Ruth had spent at least ten years with Naomi, before Ruth's husband died. It was their responsibility to care for her. There was something about Naomi which Ruth was dedicated. She saw something in her that she loved, something that she respected and something that she felt she wanted to be connected with (see Ruth1:16-17). Maybe it was Naomi's lifestyle or the way she showed strength in her loss. By doing so, with those words of dedication and duty, Ruth deconstructs herself so that she can rebuild a new.

We find other people who inspire us, we laugh and joke and say "I want to be just like you when I grow up." We have daughters who imitate us. They want to wear our shoes and dress up in our clothes, play in our make up and if you are blessed, they see something in you that they desire to have in themselves when they grow up. We find others outside of our families who we respect, honor and love which we may attempt to imitate. There are women that I have respected in the church, on my job and even in my home that I wonder, "what is her story?" I wonder how they got to be so strong and how they learned to be who they are. There is something from them that you want to pull, knowledge you would like to gain and lessons you would like to learn. How would you gain it? By breaking down what you saw and examining all the aspects of it before you try.

Deconstruction

When I look at the roles that women play in life and how we operate in them, with some I see, we have been looking at this thing all wrong. We have gotten our models from television and looking inside the lives of others. The first models were the ones we directly saw in front of us. We looked at our mothers, sisters and aunts, figuring if we wanted to be just like them or nothing like them. We picked apart what they did, what they should have done and even what we would have done if we were in that same situation. We made judgments based on the information we had and when it came to our time to make it work we probably did the very same thing they did, used the information we had to work with, and did the best we could. Understanding why we do some of the stuff we do or what is expected in certain roles we take on helps to know what we are doing and makes us better at it or more accepting of it. When you deconstruct certain things, you break down what was previously built to see what materials were used to build it. When I was younger anytime my mother asked me to do anything and I asked why, I was usually told it was because she said so. I was taught not to question adults and just do as I was told. With that, you are not learning all that you should about the task you are taking on. Yes, you are learning obedience, but obedience to what, tradition? Tradition teaches us to do certain things, because my mom did it and her mom did it. Teaching you why you are doing certain things may bring further insight on the situation and help you transition a little bit better.

I have often referred to the story of the Thanksgiving turkey, where a new wife is making her first Thanksgiving turkey and she begins to cut one of the legs off the turkey. Just then her husband walks in and asks her why she is cutting the leg off the turkey. She tells him she is doing it because her mother always did it when she cooked turkey for Thanksgiving. Her husband asked her to call her mother and ask her why she always takes off one leg of the turkey when she cooks it. The new wife calls her mother and asks her, "Why do you always cut off one leg of your Thanksgiving turkey before you cook it?" The mother then replies, "I do it because my mother did it." Her husband then advises her to call her grandmother to ask her why she cuts the leg off of the Thanksgiving turkey before she cooks it. The grandmother told her, " I cut off one leg of the Thanksgiving turkey before I cook it because my pan was too small for the whole turkey to fit!"

Repeating a tradition without knowing why you do it is not teaching you anything. Just giving you the title of wife or mother and not telling or teaching what that job entails, is setting you up for failure. Learning as much as you can about a position before entering into it will help you in the long run be the best you can be. Sometimes you have to break it down before you can build it up. In every good recipe there are instructions and directions. To make a recipe successful you must have all of the ingredients necessary to make the dish. The first thing you do is set everything out and make sure there is enough and you have the right stuff. It is not until then that you begin to mix and blend everything together. If you want to have a successful life, successful marriage or raise children successfully, look at your ingredients. Take inventory of your stock and make sure you have all the items you need before you begin blending and mixing things together.

Widow

After a few years of singleness, I was blessed to marry again. I met my second husband at my new job as an Emergency Medical Technician. We had been together for 11 years, and would have been married for ten within a few months, but he passed away when he was thirty six years old. Not only was he thirty six, so was I. I found myself young and widowed. Although my husband had multiple illnesses, I never imagined he would actually die; he was too young, I was too young, our children were too young. With my husbands Lupus, he had survived kidney failure, the amputation of three fingers, a few bouts of lung infections, a heart attack and even congestive heart failure. So when he had this little stroke, of course I thought, "Give it a few days and he will be fine." With both of us being medically trained, we knew if he made it to the hospital in time, he could receive the clot busting drug to counteract the stroke. We made it in time, the drug was given and he got eighty percent of his function back. He was going to be fine, but he wasn't fine. This was not an easy transition. I didn't know what to do. So I did the best I could. I dressed in all black, bought a few hats, lowered my skirts and hung my head. I was a widow for Pete's sake. I wasn't sure the proper protocol for mourning either. Should I only visit the cemetery weekly or daily, all holidays or just birthdays? How should I be addressed, and how should I address others. Am I still Mrs., or am I now Miss? How long should I wear my rings?

Finally I realized that some of the ways we were once connected, we were no longer. I had a new status, change had occurred and I needed to transition. When your spouse passes away, you are no longer connected to him by the bonds of marriage. _Romans 7:2 states that a woman is bound by law to her husband as long as he is alive, but should he pass away, she is released from the law of marriage._ When you took your vows with your husband, there was some through sickness and health, good and bad, respect and honor, but in the end it states, until death do you part. Many women take on the persona of the wife of their husbands. Mrs. John Jones, and when her husband passes, she continues to be Mrs. John Jones. They continue in the same fashion they were in when he was alive. Can't bring yourself to get rid of his clothes, keeping personal items, still wearing the ring, building shrines with photos and other memorabilia, and still signing your name Mrs. John Jones. All the while holding on to the connection that you once had with that person. Where in reality, the bond that you shared with that person, is now broken, and you are free. You are now single and your identity, your status and how you are identified has again changed.

In biblical times being a widow was considered a poor state. Women were not really workers and counted on their husbands for their lively hood. Should your husband die, you were to be cared for by his family. Should you be young enough and with no children, laws stated that the brother of the deceased husband was to marry his wife and give her children to carry on his name. (See Deuteronomy 5:5-6) Blessed are we that the law is no longer in effect, nothing against my brother-in-law, but the Lord only knows, I couldn't do it! During the time that Ruth became a widow, there was no one to carry on. Both of Naomi's sons had died. Naomi blessed her two daughters-in- law and attempted to send them both back home to their parents so that they would have another chance for marriage. _"May the Lord grant that each of you will find rest in the home of another husband. Ruth 1:9_ Naomi is insistent that since they are now without husbands and she cannot have another son soon enough for them to be able to care for the widows, that they were young enough to go back to their parents home and be available for another husband. There was no true reason for the young ladies to remain unmarried. Yes they loved their husbands and they truly were mourning for them, but the fact still remained that the bond that was once there was lost. Naomi's other daughter-in-law decided that it was best for her to return and try it again. That was her choice. No one can tell you when the right time is for you to transition from your loss. No one can tell you when enough time has passed for your grieving process or when it's a good time to remarry or not. There will be different things that will help you to determine how long or if you remain single. That should be decided by you and God. .

It is not easy to transition from married, back to single, through death being the loss you experience. Knowing and understanding that you are free from the bond will help make the transition easier. You cannot feel guilty or feel as if you are cheating your deceased spouse should you move into a newness of life. You are not forgetting him, you are just remembering you. Challenges will rise and lonely times will come, so Jesus promised us the Holy Spirit: *and I will ask the Father and he will give you another Counselor to be with you forever. John 14:16.* Moving on does not take away from the love you shared, the Holy Spirit will help ease the pain and assist in your transitional period.

Single

What makes you single? The simple fact that you are not married. If you are widowed, you are single. Even if you have a boo, even if you are playing house with your live in lover, even if he is your baby's daddy, if you are not married, you are single. Single is a state of mind and it is a state of being. It is what it is. Justifying your relationship for more than it is to fit your designated status is not only inappropriate, it is just plain old biblically wrong. We make certain significations stating that we have been together for a long time, we go together or we are a couple. We mix our finances and all, and by worldly standards, that is a good argument, but biblically, you don't have a leg to stand on. We have let go of the biblical stand of the appropriateness of a relationship and allowed the world to dictate the dynamics of it. So it stands to reason that you have adopted this lifestyle and believe that it is ok, but yet that small voice inside of you knows that it is not a Godly relationship. We stay in these relationships because we feel as if we are attached, or have become connected by the finances we have combined and the children that have come about and the families we have brought together and in all of that. In reality you are just two separate entities with all this stuff and if you are not married, you are still single. As stated before, some people choose to be single, choose never to share their lives with another person for one reason or another. It is a choice.

As long as you choose to remain single, in which ever situation you are in, there are yet certain guidelines you should attempt to follow, and oh it will be a sacrifice! *I beseech you therefore, brethren, by the mercies of God, that ye present your bodies a living sacrifice, holy, acceptable unto God, which is your reasonable service.* Romans 12:1 (KJV)

A sacrifice was given and brought to the temple or priest to be killed and placed on the alter as a blessing to the Lord. God no longer wants dead sacrifices, but he does want us to die to our flesh and sacrifice of yourself, for his will to be done. Commitment to God is the greatest sacrifice you could give, and it's not all that unreasonable. As you present yourself holy and pleasing to God, you are setting yourself apart from things that would cause you to be unholy. Respecting your mind and your body is a number one way of accomplishing this. The priest would not accept any sacrifice that was not of its best, no foul or unclean animal was accepted into the temple. Why would you accept any thing foul or unclean in your temple? It should be unacceptable. Marking up your bodies with the names of people, places and things and putting substances into your bodies that take away your natural spirit. Allowing persons to speak foul language or bring unclean items into your mind or body, all unacceptable.

The second verse of that same scripture reminds us not to be conformed to the things of this world, but to renew your mind and be transformed, that you may be able to prove what is good and acceptable in the perfect will of God. Renewing and transforming your mind goes hand and hand. If you gain new knowledge and it does not change you, you have missed something. You cannot live the same life you were living, do the same thing you were doing and expect to be rewarded. Give up the things of the world and set your mind on things that are of Christ, because only what you do for Christ will last. When you have sacrificed yourself for God and you are Holy and pleasing to him, you are set apart for the work of Gods kingdom. That could mean becoming a part of the body of Christ, working in the church, ministering to lost souls, preaching the gospel or even being set apart to under gird a man of God, being set apart for the duty and service of marriage. How you transition into the role of a married person will take new skills.

There are some areas that you must leave behind during the transition. Taking some single skills into a marriage relationship will be beneficial, some will not. You cannot take a single person's mentality into a married relationship because it's not just about you anymore. One of the first roles you should adopt even as a single person is submission. I know, some of you think that should have been a bad word, but in reality it's a biblical principle that's not that hard to grasp. Everyone is under some type of authority, whether on your job, in your home under your parents, or in your church. Even the highest authority, still must fall under submission. *Everyone must submit himself to the governing authorities, for there is no authority except that which God has established. The authorities that exist have been established by God. Consequently, he who rebels against the authority is rebelling against what God has instituted, and those who do so will bring judgment on themselves. Romans 13:1-2* When the centurion solider in Matthew chapter eight asked Jesus to help his servant by healing him, the centurion told Him that he didn't even deserve Jesus to come with him under his roof. He advised Jesus that he was a man under authority himself, and yet still had people under his authority, but he believed that Jesus only had to speak the word and heal his servant. Jesus told him that He had never seen someone with such faith, and because of his faith, he would heal his servant. You have to have the faith that God will bless you with a covenant marriage relationship before he makes it so. In your faith you must trust him enough to begin the transformation and begin to submit before the time comes. Submit unto God as your present authority until he replaces that with the covenant authority of a husband that is submitting unto Him. He may have already spoken the word concerning your future, have the faith to receive it. He may just be waiting on you. As a single woman you may have taken on other roles, one of which is a role of independence. There is truly nothing wrong with being independent and self reliant, but once you have been set apart for marriage you must transition from your independent life, to now become part of another.

Married

Someplace between the proposal and the day after the wedding, the concept of marriage has been lost. There has been some misconception about the importance of a wedding and the importance of a marriage. People come together with their families and friends, sit down and plan for the event, but never plan for their lives. They put more emphasis on the wedding day than married life. Emphasis gets placed on having a church wedding but not having a saved marriage. In reality, an average wedding from start to finish takes 30 minutes, putting all of the emphasis on that day instead of the marriage may make it last the same amount of time. There have been some misconceptions and the focus has been changed to senses of entitlement for "my big day." When in reality, the focus should be on "our peaceful lives." The covenant of marriage is a holy one, not one to be entered into lightly. A covenant is a promise that is made between you and the person you stand with, the person you say that you love, and who you are choosing to spend your life with. Reality TV and commercialism have made marriage about the bride, saying it's "her" day, focusing on the dress, the flowers, the cake and the venue. What about the vows, and what about the duties of the couple? Where does that fit? That is the time to be mindful of your promise and the covenant you are entering into.

There are so many scriptures defining the duties, and importance of wives and husbands. Too many for this book. Just know that no one scripture tells you everything you need to know about being a wife or what is expected. If you ever have any questions, that is where you should look, understand the times and culture that it was written, the basis of Gods plan for the wife is described in the beginning of the bible. After the creation of man and woman, and the serpent's crafty ways corrupted them, God handed down his punishment to Adam and Eve. *To the woman he said, "I will greatly increase your pains in childbearing; with pain you will give birth to children. Your desire will be for your husband, and he will rule over you." Genesis 3:16*

This is where the authority was given, in the beginning, but right before that, God cursed woman with the desire for her husband. Wow, what a curse. I have wondered time and time again why women love so hard, why we take so much, and why we will do anything for our husbands. It is because we are cursed with a desire. Sometimes it seems the pain of childbirth is more bearable, but it's what we have to contend with. Because God loves us, this is the punishment we must deal with. He could have killed us and not allowed us any mercy. When you begin to examine the reasoning and the intent for marriage, your role should not be that hard to transition into. Understanding that it is not about the dress, it is not about the size of the ring and it is not about what everybody else thinks, you will be giving your marriage the proper consideration. A marriage relationship is not about what you are and are not going to do. A marriage relationship is not about who is supposed to do what. If you choose to share your life with someone, that was a conscious choice that you made to share every aspect, every part and every position of your life with this other person. It may not be 50-50 all the time. There may be times in your marriage relationship where you must carry eighty percent of the load while he can only carry twenty. There may be times where he may carry seventy percent and you only carry thirty. When you bring them together, it will still make that 100. He may not do it like you would do it, but allow him to do his part the way he knows how and he will be willing to give a bigger percent next time. When you stand and make a commitment with this other person, you don't know what will happen in the future, but you are stating that you are willing to accept it and deal with it. There should be no tit for tat in marriage. When you give, give out of love, caring and understanding that you are giving because it pleases you to give and when you receive, receive with compassion understanding that someone is trying to please you. Don't expect to receive any more than you are willing to give. Give more than you expect to receive. If the both of you do that, you will have more than enough. Don't expect him to be as you are but allow him to bring his originality to the relationship and mesh the two together. There was something about him that made you want to make him a permanent part of you life. Marriage has connected you in a bond, don't live it in bondage. It is a true commitment. Don't live by the rules of the world, figure out what you are willing to commit to and what works for the two of you, then do it. Be clear about your decisions and your actions.

CHAPTER 3   Conversion

Harvest Time

So Naomi returned, and Ruth the Moabitess, her daughter in law, with her, which returned out of the country of Moab; and they came to Bethlehem in the beginning of the barley harvest. Ruth 1:22

There is a certain agricultural significance to the principle of sowing and reaping. Sowing is considered planting a seed. The seed is the original beginning of the crop to which you are to grow. The reaping comes after the seed has been sown into the fertile ground, and the plant has yielded a crop. That is when you are able to receive the harvest from the plant. There is another process that must occur before the plant even begins to grow to where you may see any yield at all. The seed that you plant is very small, but the crop that it yields is much larger. Should you plant a seed of corn, it takes some time in the ground to take root. It then begins to mix with the soil and the things that are in the soil that makes it stronger and richer before it peaks its head from out of the dirt. There are other periods of growth which take place over time before the plant is ready to be harvested by the reapers. When it is ready to be harvested, instead of just a seed, you have a whole plant. More than just a seed, more than just one piece of fruit or vegetable or what ever it is that you have planted. It comes back with much more. These women were coming from a situation of lack, a circumstance of loss and feeling bitter. But they came into a harvest. The barley harvest was immediately after the winter and the first crops were usually ready for harvest in the middle of April or early May. By the time of this harvest, the rains have already come and gone, the storms have passed over and now it is time to gather what was previously sown a time ago. Now you would think, what does this have to do with Naomi and Ruth? They didn't sow any seeds here so why would they reap any of the harvest? This is why you have to be mindful of who you associate yourself with. Naomi knew that her state, although poor, although bitter, still left her certain assistances.

I have always enjoyed gardening. There was a time when I used to say that I had a black thumb because whatever I planted or any plant that I attempted to care for would die. I never knew if I watered it too much, gave it too much light or possibly didn't care for it enough and it lacked the attention needed to live. I still have not mastered house plants but should I have a small plot of ground, a garden I will plant. Starting off with seeds was always interesting to me because I loved to see the process of growth in the plants and what would become of them. From preparing the ground, to picking out the clumps, to watering, digging, and ultimately planting the seeds, to the first peak of the plant coming above the dirt was a task. Daily checking on the progress and even after the first sight of life, now the next stage, the budding of the flower and the emerging of the actual vegetable, its growth and the preparation for picking it, the whole time is an exciting process for me. Some of the time the things I planted, I never even intended on eating. I just wanted to watch it grow. It wouldn't be wasted though, it would be given to someone else as well as all of the remainder of whatever else I was growing that my family wouldn't consume. It blesses me to watch it grow and it blesses someone else to receive what has been grown that can feed and nurture their bodies and spirits.

Even though Naomi and Ruth never planted anything in this particular field, there was a way that they could receive from the harvest that could nurture their bodies and bless their spirits. *And let us not be weary in well doing; for in due season we reap, if we faint not. Galatians 6:9 (KJV)* Sometimes it is hard work to sow into someone's life especially when you don't seem to be getting anything in return. But it's not necessarily going to be the return you may be anticipating. You may plant a seed of understanding but your harvest may come in wisdom. You may sow finances and your harvest come years later in the form of a paid scholarship for one of your children. When Naomi allowed Ruth to come with her, she planted a seed with Ruth that there would need to be a season of growth before the harvest. Naomi planted now as she sowed into the life of Ruth by helping her. She helped Ruth renew her life from the devastation of loss. After the period of growth she would later receive the harvest from her sowing. We have so much good seed that we can plant into the lives of others. Let God do the watering and pruning, then watch the growing and the harvest come forth.

Stages

Recently where I live, there was a serious storm that caused a flood in areas and neighborhoods which were not actually in flood plains or low lying areas. Due to lack of care with the drainage systems in those areas, total neighborhoods became overwhelmed by rain waters and flooded. After the waters receded, there was a lot of damage and a lot of loss. Personal and irreplaceable belongings like vehicles, furniture, photos and memorabilia were completely destroyed. There was even illness and disease caused by the contaminated water. The storm was over, the rain had come and gone, and as the people looked around and they began to wonder. What is next? What do we do now? How do we deal with this loss? Anytime you suffer a loss of any kind, you must learn how to deal with it. Whether it is the loss of a home, job, loved one, friendship or relationship, it is still a loss, and must be dealt with because you will need to grieve. Grief is defined as a deep distress brought on by suffering or some type of unfortunate outcome and it is a process that each one of us will go through. It will help if you go through the process one step at a time. There are five stages of grief which people are prone to go through. You may not go through them in any particular order and you may stay in one stage longer than you do the next, but at some point you must go through these stages.

Transitioning through the process of grieving will help you in the next area of your life or should the same ever apply again. Sometimes the stages of grief take a while to transition through, and sometimes you feel all of the emotions immediately. Accept them and deal with them. You cannot change what happened nor can you force yourself to move to the next stage before you are ready. There is a different way to look at these stages. By looking at an alternate way to go through this process, you will see that it may make it a little bit easier to transition.

- **Denial**

In reading the beginning of Naomi and Ruth's stories, it doesn't show that either of the ladies immediately acknowledged the death of their husbands. Maybe Naomi didn't feel she had time to mourn. This story tells nothing of burials, grieving or her state of mind. Naomi went on with her life and the task she had to accomplish. Naomi's loss did not begin with the deaths in her family. It began when she originally left her homeland, the land of promise and left her family and friends. Naomi's husband had taken the family to another place away from their home land. While they were there he died; the story says nothing of her grieving, then ten years later, her sons also died. After the deaths of her husband and sons, Naomi's next move was to go back home where she came from because the reason they left was no longer an issue. In reality, she moved back home for the same reason she left, she again was experiencing lack. Loss does not only come from death. Loss comes from anything you once had, that you have no more. Often times, when we experience some type of loss, we go on with our lives as if we must just get to the next task. Oh I lost my job, guess I have to get another one, I lost my pregnancy, we will just try it again. We live with the "get up and dust yourself off mentality", which is fine, when you can acknowledge the reason you fell in the first place. There has been a change or a shift and it must be dealt with because this is the beginning of a new transition. When I found out my husband passed away, I was leaving work. It was a job I had just begun the week of his stroke. I continued to go to work daily until I was told by my new boss to stay home. I was thinking "if I just kept myself busy enough", "if I found enough to do", I wouldn't have to think about it and it wouldn't hurt so much. I was in denial. Throwing yourself into task after task, duty after duty and job after job will not change the fact that something has occurred in your life and you need to deal with it.

Acting like it never occurred will not help you transition, it will mentally, keep you in that same place of loss. You can not go through life ignoring things that happen to you or covering them up with denial. Denial is saying that you are ok, when you really are not. Denial is saying that you can handle it alone and you really cannot. Denial is acting like nothing really happened, and it did. Acknowledging that this thing did really happen, or it is really happening, and facing what you must, will help you get through this process. Instead of denying something happened, deal with what happened.

- **Deal**

The first thing you must do when you discover a loss is to deal with the loss. What happened, why did it happen, how did it happen and what can I learn from what happened should be some of your first questions. Once you begin to find answers to these questions you can begin to deal with them accordingly. Emotions will play a big part in how you deal with your loss, pain, pressure or distance. You must say, "this is what has happened, now what am I going to do about it?" Dealing with it may be confronting the loss or the cause of the loss. It may be forgiving the parties involved or even accepting immediately what has occurred. Confrontation is not always a negative or volatile thing. To confront something just means to come face to face with it. You may not be able to come face to face with the actual person or the actual item, but you can face the situation. You may think you are dealing with it because you did it in your "own way." But have you really dealt with it? Covering it up, is not dealing with it. Pushing it aside, is not dealing with it. Internalizing it is not dealing with it. You have to face that thing no matter how bad it hurts and see it for what it is and what it was. Talk to it. Talk to someone about it. You may need to write a letter or write it in the sky, but you need to let it out so you can get away from it. Figure out the best way for you to deal with it. One way that works for one, may not work for the other. So find out what works for you and work it. You may have to remind yourself each day to get rid of one thing. You may have to teach yourself a mantra, repeating positive things to keep you moving. Just find something that works for you. If you find that months or years later that it still hurts the same and thinking about it takes you back to the initial pain, you still have not dealt with it.

- **Anger**

When the women departed Moab, they all were going together, to the same destination at the same time. At some point, Naomi decided she didn't want the women to go with her (see Ruth 1:11-13). She told each of them to go back to their parent's home and find another husband. After she explained why they should not come with her she made a statement of accusation that the Lord's hand had gone out against her. She blamed God for her loss and took this as a personal attack from him. Naomi had experienced much loss and she did not know the reason why it had happened to her so she began pushing the women away from her.

When we are angry at a situation or circumstance of loss, we don't feel as if people understand what we are going through or dealing with and we become angry. Even though we may be angry at the situation we take it out on the persons closest to us. We even become angry with the person who passed away sighting reason after reason. "They should not have been there." "They should have taken better care of themselves." "How dare they leave me here alone?" We even become angry at God. "How could he let this happen?" We begin to question His motives.

For we wrestle not against flesh and blood, but against principalities, against powers, against the rulers of the darkness of this world, against spiritual wickedness in high places. Ephesians 6:12 (KJV) Principalities are the beginning of the issues you are fighting against. They are root of the problem. The person may not be at fault for the loss and your anger must be directed to the appropriate place. Oh I was angry, I was upset and I was just down right in despair. I could not believe that he had left me all alone with our children. My youngest was just four at the time. He made me go through the worst shopping excursion of my life, picking out caskets, flowers, clothing and paper stock. For months I walked around angry at him and angry at my family and friends. They didn't understand, so they left me alone out of fear of hurting me more. They didn't know what to say or how to act, so they said nothing and acted like nothing had happened. I began to lash out until finally my best friend and my niece told me that I was being very, very mean. I didn't even realize my behavior had changed. I was acting the way I felt.

You have to be careful not to misdirect or hold onto blame like security. There may not be anyone to blame for what has occurred. Allow yourself to feel the emotion of anger but carefully think about the direction you take.

- **Allowance**

I could no longer sit and be angry, I had to move on. I wrote a letter to my husband, telling him how angry I was. I went to the cemetery, sat down on the ground near his grave, read him the letter and after a few tears, I left. I have gone back to the cemetery on many occasions, but I came to realize that my husband was no longer there. There is nothing wrong with being angry. You just have to deal with your anger in the proper manner.*) Be angry, and sin not: let not the sun go down upon your wrath: Neither give place to the devil. Ephesians 4:26-27 (KJV* Allow yourself to be angry, just direct it in the proper place. When you allow yourself to feel emotions, you allow yourself the freedom to process the event. You actually give yourself the chance to feel what you should be feeling and it may not have the opportunity to manifest into anger. When we get angry the first thing we want to do is react and we don't think about the effect of our reaction. Reaction is described as any response caused by some other event. When we react we may loose control. People love to tell you not to be angry over a situation or over a loss, but anger is a natural response in some events of loss. It is ok to allow yourself to feel how you feel. But you have to get to a point in your stage and your situation where you see yourself as a survivor and not a victim. Envision yourself in a place which is on the other side of the problem or the other side of the pain. "Yes, this did happen but I'm still here." "Yes, he is gone, but I still have my children." "Yes I am able to deal with this in the most positive way imaginable." The way you allow yourself to feel may help someone else who goes through the same thing.

- **Bargaining**

When I think of bargaining I think of the old TV show "Let's Make a Deal," where you have something that I want and I will give you what I have to get it. Naomi attempted to bargain with her daughter-in-laws, telling them to go back home because she had nothing for them. She told them that if they went back home, they could get new husbands. When one decided to go back, she tells the other look, she's going back, go with her. Ruth even began to bargain with Naomi, not to send her back. Ruth tells Naomi *"Where you go I will go, and were you stay I will stay. Your people will be my people and your God my God. Where you die I will die, and there I will be buried. May the LORD deal with me, be it ever so severely, if anything but death separates you and me"* Ruth 1:16-17

Ruth is offering her dedication to Naomi for the opportunity to go with her. By telling Naomi, "I will allow the same Lord that you say dealt bitterly with you, if you let me go with you. I'll let that same Lord deal bitterly with me. If you let me go with you, ill serve your God, if you let me go with you, I'll live where you live." Let's make a deal. We try to play "Let's Make a Deal" with God when we suffer loss. We start making promises we can't possibly keep. "Lord if you just bring him back, you can take me! Really! Lord I'll stop doing everything that I was doing if you just give me that relationship back. Lord if you save me I will come to church every Sunday. I'll be good if you bless me." You can not make deals with God, or with others and offer false hope. Instead of offering a bargain, try a new beginning.

• **Beginning**

If you look at the terms of your bargain attempts, they may give you an idea of a way to begin again. As Ruth pledged her self to Naomi with everything that she said, she was not only looking at a new beginning, she realized that something for her had ended. She realized that she didn't want to go back to what she had before. If your bargain is to stop doing something in order to get something back, maybe you should stop doing it to get something new? You may not know the reason for that one thing ending but you can understand that it is an opportunity for a new beginning. When we look at loss we only see what has gone and it's hard to view what is coming. When looking at a new beginning, you must look ahead. This is the middle of your transition, you have already gone in the right direction and you cannot turn back. You may not be able to see what is ahead, but if you keep moving forward, as you begin to come out, you can gain insight to a new beginning.

• Depression

"It is more bitter for me than for you, because the Lord's hand has gone out against me!" Ruth 1:13, One thing after another, she moved from her home land, her husband died, her sons died, now she has no one to take care of her and she has to get back home. "Woe is me!" Depression can set in from a loss and after a series of other events which may occur by not dealing with the loss. Like not allowing yourself to be angry and not visualizing a new beginning and feeling powerless against the event. Many feelings and emotions begin to flow. You may begin to feel guilt, remorse and many other emotions because you don't feel like you can get past this present predicament. To be in a depressed state is to be in a low state of mind and having a low ability to function.

Naomi began to feel sorry for herself and states that her condition is worse than the condition of the other two. But haven't they all suffered a loss? I have only known one other young woman personally to lose her husband at my age and that was my best friend. Is my loss greater than hers because I have kids? Was my loss greater than the loss his mother experienced? What about his brother's loss? What about the loss my kids must now deal with? Is my loss any greater than theirs? Feeling alone and that no one understands is a common thing, but there is no new thing under the sun. Everything you are experiencing, someone else may have already experienced it. Don't deal with this by yourself. Share your story, express yourself and do what you can to assist aide in coming out of this state of mind.

- **Deliverance**

When something is conceived in you such as loss and you begin to go through the stages of grief, you begin a process of allowing the growth of something that can only be removed from your spirit by deliverance. Once something has taken root, grown and developed, it begins to take up too much space, pushing some things out of the way and suffocating others. It becomes too big when you cannot function in your day to day life, work, be the mother, sister or friend. There comes a time when it must be removed and even delivery is a process. When I think of deliverance or being delivered I think of a woman having a baby and the entire process of labor, the pains, the pushing and the production of something beautiful as the outcome. There are many ways of being delivered, not just one. You may be delivered prematurely and the growth is not complete. You may be delivered pain-free where you got through the process without being hurt or hurting anyone. Or you may be delivered with the help of an outside source which helps take the pain away. Some deliveries may leave scars, marks or bruises while some deliveries will be so easy, that you may not have any reminders left behind. No matter how long you carry this thing, eventually you need to allow it to come out of you. You may have to labor long and hard or it may be an easy transition. Either way when it is born, when it is released from you, you shall rejoice, for the end of one stage and the beginning of another. Recovery. After your deliverance, take the time to recover physically, mentally and spiritually.

- **Acceptance**

(Ruth 1:18) When Naomi realized that Ruth was determined to go with her, she stopped urging her. This is the point where either, we have gotten too tired to fight, or we realize that it is not our fight anymore. Acceptance does not necessarily mean that you agree with the circumstance or the event. It just means that you have come to some comprehensible terms about it. You no longer deny it, are angered by it or allow it to depress you. And you no longer fight against it. Naomi came to terms with the fact that her husband was gone, her sons were gone. Widowed, this was the state she was in. She also understood that there was someone else in a condition similar to hers who was also in need. It was at that point that Naomi realized it was not just about her. She was not the only one who had a painful event in her life. There was nothing she could do to change what had occurred, but she could look forward to what may occur in their lives.

- **Anticipation**

This is a way to be excited about what is to come. A lot of times during the grieving period when we get to the end, we find a way to find pleasure out of what got us to this point. We begin to remember the good things about the person who passed. We begin to have happy memories of the things which we once had and find pleasure in what used to be. It is also a time where we find hope again and realize that even though the event occurred, because we are still here, because God allowed us to remain, because he gave us another chance, we have something to look forward to. No matter what the loss, no matter what event caused the loss, God knows what he is doing.) *and we know that all things work together for good to them that love God, to them who are the called according to his purpose. Romans 8:28 (KJV)* It may not seem like it is happening for your good but my Lord and your God has made us more than conquerors over any enemy we face.

Picking up the pieces

When you get to the end of your storm, you find that you have fought all you can fight, you have gone through all of the stages of grief from your losses and you have gone down as far as you can go. What do you next? Your next move is to pick up the left over pieces of your life, put them all together and see what you can make of them. Once Naomi and Ruth made it to a stable place, Ruth asked Naomi to allow her to go out into the fields and pick up left over grain. This was considered gleaning. Owners of fields were required by law to leave the corners of their fields from the harvest untouched so that the poor, widows, and people in need could come and gather crops to use for themselves (See Leviticus 23:22). This would help in a number of ways, it would stop some people from begging for help from others and it would help build a supply for people in need. Ruth realized there must be a next step, and this is the one she took. Getting up, going to work by picking up what is left over. By getting up, getting out of the home, going to work, making herself productive she was affirming worthiness to herself and to Naomi.

Some people think leftovers are unworthy of a second look. After all, it is what is left after you have gotten all that you want or need. It is not what has been chosen or what has been used. Leftovers have been set aside, and set apart from the rest. If you never realized it before, that is a blessing in itself. Don't you see that if there is something left over, that means there is extra! That means that you have more than enough and now there is surplus. It has not been touched and it hasn't been used.

There are parts of our lives we look at as leftovers. Some of us look at ourselves as leftovers. We were passed over for a promotion, or not picked for an important task we thought was definitely for us. Some look at themselves as unwanted, unneeded and unworthy, but don't you realize that you have been blessed, set aside and set apart to be picked up and used in another way? It may not be the way that you originally intended, but that doesn't mean you are not set for a task. Pick up the pieces of your life you have put aside for whatever reason. When you find yourself in the position to get up and go out, begin to make those things useful. Ruth didn't wait on someone to come and knock on the door and offer assistance. She didn't wait on someone to come and take care of them. She took initiative and got to work. There are so many aspects of our lives which we have left in the corner of the field or placed on the back burners of our mind. Even things on the back burner still need tending. Now may be the time to go back to school, volunteer your services, write a book, start that ministry or open that business. Begin to incorporate other things, other activities and other people into your life.

It just so happened

As it turned out, she found herself working in a field belonging to Boaz, who was from the clan of Elimelech. Ruth 2:3

Have you ever been driving down the street and end up on the other side of town? Or you are walking through the store and you run into someone you have not seen in a long time? Maybe you were just sitting at home and someone stopped by or gave you a phone call, where at some point you are saying or thinking, it just so happened that I was on this side of town, or I just so happened to run into Sister So and So, or maybe as it happened you just found yourself being blessed by these occurrences. Well nothing just happens. Through the assignment of the Holy Spirit and the appointment of God, you just met your "divine appointment" and you were right on time. It was not a mistake and it was not an accident that you where you were when you got blessed or that you saw who you saw who blessed you. You were trying to pump gas at the station you always go to and for some reason the pumps didn't work today. You are irritated and frustrated, but you leave anyway and go to the next station up the road. It just so happens that an old high school friend works at this station and she has been looking for you for a long time. After you all reconnect and reminisce you realize that there was a reason for you all meeting back up. That was a divine appointment, something that either you or that person has been praying for or that your spirit has been longing for and God has heard you. When Ruth left home requesting to go into the fields she asked for favor (see Ruth 2:2). As she began to work, she just happened to be in the field of the relative of her Mother-in-law. It just so happened that she was in the field of Boaz and he noticed her working in the corner of the field. Not knowing for sure what drew his attention to her, (her beauty or her diligence), she was in the right place at the right time to be blessed. One bible story that helps me when I cannot see my blessing and strengthens me with my faith in others and the divine appointment of God is the conversion of Saul to Paul. Relatively known as his Damascus Road Experience (Acts 9:1-22). There was one that was praying for a blessing and another who heard the voice of God on how to be a blessing. God knows where you are, and He knows who you are. He hears your prayers and He hears you calling out to Him. He heard Saul and he will hear you. Now it is up to his people to be obedient to his call. They don't have to agree with it, just be obedient to it. It will just happen that you are on the same road, or in the same field, or on the same job, or in the same church as the person who is to be a blessing in your life. When God speaks into your spirit to be a blessing, you should be obedient to that call. Use a discerning spirit to get to your appointment. You don't know what that praying person has been praying to Him. Your obedience could be helping a person out of a bind. That knock on the door may stop that suicidal spirit from entering in, and that phone call you make may ease the troubled mind of someone thinking no one cares. Allow God to use you in a way that it Just So Happens you are in the right place at the right time not only to be blessed, but maybe to be a blessing.

CHAPTER 4   Character Concerns

Just then Boaz arrived from Bethlehem and greeted the harvesters, "The LORD be with you!" "The LORD bless you!" they called back Ruth 2:4

We have all been in a new place at one time or another. New to us, but maybe not to others surrounding us. Starting a new job, going to a new church, being introduced as a new family member are some of the new situations we can find ourselves in. You had better believe that someone there knows something about you. Even though you are new, someone has been speaking about you. Now whether it is the truth or what they think they know, someone knows something, and if asked, they will tell. But when they say what they know, what will they be saying about you? How will they describe your character (Ruth 2:7, 11-12)? The foreman went on to explain not only what he had heard about her, he told Boaz what he had observed of her. The foreman told him that Ruth had worked hard from the time she had gotten there up until that moment, except for a short rest. When Boaz approached Ruth, he told her, "I've heard what you have done, how you left your own family to care for someone in mine. I have heard how you have unselfishly given up your quest for a new life, to assist someone else in reclaiming theirs. I have heard how you have left your home, your people and your gods to come here as a stranger and gain a new life. I have heard all of these things about you before I even met you."

What are people hearing about you? What are people saying about you when you are not around? People don't only discuss you negatively when you are not around. Sometimes people speak kindly of you, of your deeds and your works. What are you doing that could make your name great among God's people? One thing that my Pastor says which I love is, "dogs don't bark at parked cars." If you are sitting still, nobody has a reason to notice you. But if you are moving and doing something, it will get the attention of those sitting on the sidelines. There are plenty of positive things that you can do to gain attention. Ruth's character of being a caring, compassionate, hard worker had preceded her. People knew who she was, who she was connected to and what kind of love she showed to others because of her works. Her character was in her works. If you remember where she was from, you would look at her a little bit funny. If you look at her state of being a widow, poor and working in the corners of the field you wouldn't think very highly of her. When man looks on the outside, God looks on the inside and her character spoke for her. I'm not sure when Ruth's conversion took place. It could have taken place when she came to the family seeing the strength of Naomi, upon the loss of her husband or it could have taken place on the road to Bethlehem along side Naomi. No one may have been witness to the act, but they were witness to her new actions. Some will not be accepting of the change in your character which occurs. Who else knows that better than Paul during his Damascus Road Experience? Before Ananias was obedient to God in going to bless him, Ananias questioned God saying, "isn't that the same man that was persecuting your people?"

People are still going to question the change that you are attempting to make. "Isn't that the same girl who has all those kids by different men," or "isn't that the same lady that has been married all of those times?" Take note from Paul, time after time he was questioned about his conversion, and he would explain time after time about how his experience brought him to Christ. His story didn't change and he didn't waiver. Some believed and some trusted that his character was different from before. Soon some started to tell his story for him. His testimony had touched others and they understood. Don't be ashamed to tell your story, someone needs to hear it. As he worked and as he spoke and as he preached what he had previously persecuted, more and more people believed. His bad character had preceded him, then after his conversion, so did his good character.

Knowing his role

Considering, up to this point we have been discussing women, identifying our identities, knowing our roles and building our characters, is it not as important to recognize, identify and characterize the man of God who we desire for our lives?

In biblical times and still in certain countries today, marriages were arranged and relationships were formed with the family and not the couple. Families found mates within their own family units, keeping the finances and the economic status within the family. When I think of it, it makes a little sense to me. You are already familiar with your relatives, you share the same back ground and you pretty much already know a lot about this person.

If I could just have a sidebar for a moment and inform all of the women in the world today, when a man first sees a woman and decides that he wants that woman, it is not because he knows about her cooking and cleaning skills. That is not the initial attraction. Initial attraction is physical, purely physical from the color of her skin, the shape of her body, the style of her hair and the clothes that she wears.

Purely physical. There are few instances where relationships begin from friendship or from another area, but generally speaking......physical attraction is where it begins. When you decide to move forward into a relationship and you realize that this is the person you are being chosen by, there are still certain qualities this person should possess. Once he looks past the initial attraction, there are other qualities he expects for you to have as well when he begins to look for a mate. What are the qualities you expect him to possess?

Security

When you ask a group of women what they look for in a husband, the initial response is security or stability. For such a short statement, it covers a vast area. Security or stability in what? Secure and stable in one area is not necessarily secure and stable in all. There are financial securities and spiritual securities. Would you like him to be mentally stable, and physically stable? What about secure in an economic position on his job or in his career or maybe come from a stable family back ground? What about secure in his religious beliefs where he cannot be swayed? Yeah, all of that sounds good doesn't it? If you will be able to find all of that stability in one person will be a blessing. Maybe he will be stable in areas that you are not and you will balance each other out. Boaz was a man of character and a man of good standing in the community. When brought up in conversation by Naomi, she expressed that to Ruth. This was the character of Boaz that preceded him. There were certain things that were known of Boaz and his character. Boaz was a business owner, whose field, Ruth found herself in when she was gleaning. Ruth had heard about the qualities that Boaz possessed and there would come a time that she would be privy to them as a witness.

Think back to when you first met your husband. What was he doing and where was he? What type of atmosphere was he in? How was he responding to others? What did you hear about him? Were others praising him?

Ruth's first encounter with Boaz was at his place of business. The first thing that Boaz did when he arrived on the scene was offer a blessing to his workers (Ruth 2:4) the way that they offered a return blessing to him. This lets me know that this was a common practice between them. If the person that you are with is not kind to others, how do you really expect him to treat you? How does he treat his mother? How does he treat other women in his own family? Should he have no compassion or no concern of how he treats others? Your special treatment is only conditional. Not only did he offer blessings to his workers, once he found out who Ruth was, he offered personal blessings to her (see Ruth 2:12). Can the man in your life pray for you? He is your covering. It is his duty to cover you in prayer and the blessings of God. Make sure you feel secure in his dedication to you and stable in the situations which come about in your relationship. Trust enough in him to protect you making you feel safe not only physically, but emotionally, spiritually and provisionally.

Physical Protection

The security of protection is also a great source of stability that women like to feel. Knowing that you have got me, you have got my back and I don't have to worry about anyone doing something to me, is a very rewarding feeling. It has been told that during a wedding ceremony, the woman is supposed to stand on the left side of the man because you were leaving his strongest hand, his fighting hand free. Should you be walking hand and hand with your husband and you all were approached by danger, he could protect you with his left hand and still have his strong fighting hand free to attack. We all look for that knight in shining armor to protect us. Come and sweep us off of our feet, protecting us from all danger, keeping us from harm and taking us away from all of the danger at hand. He may not come in on a big black stallion while dressed in polished armor but you will know if you have been rescued or if you have been fed to the wolves. Protecting you from danger is more than pushing you out of the way of a speeding car. Although heroic, can he discern the spirit of someone trying to use you or can he speak to your spirit about making good decisions about your life? Can he assist you in the position you are working in without trying to get anything in return? Boaz asked nothing of Ruth, but he still showed concern for her care.

So Boaz said to Ruth, "My daughter, listen to me. Don't go and glean in another field and don't go away from here. Stay here with my servant girls. Watch the field where you are harvesting, and follow along after the girls. I have told the men not to touch you. Ruth 2:8-9a

    Boaz offered her physical security; protecting her from all of the other men that were out in the fields. There was a certain danger that Ruth was in being out there all alone. She was an alien, and a widow, but he offered her protection. You should be secure in the fact that your mate has your back, that he has your best interest at heart. That means he is not himself, doing things to damage you. He cannot protect you physically and harm you physically at the same time. That means he is not abusive physically or mentally. He is not harming you with words, and he is protecting you from the harsh words of others. I have heard time and time again women asking their husbands, "are you going to let them speak to me that way?" I'm not telling you that he should jump and attack anyone that speaks to you in a bad way or hurts your feelings, but he should be protective of your feelings and not partake in the bashing and not partake in the tearing down of your self-esteem.

Now ladies, don't get your husband into a physical altercation with someone because you know he has your back and you cannot manage your mouth. Yes, we have an expectation of care, but sometimes we can get ourselves into some stuff, that we want them to get us out. When Boaz told the other men that she was off limits, the reason they left her alone was out of respect for him, not her. There should be a character of your husband, which some people would not even step your way with anything out of line. Men would not approach you with anything inappropriate because they respect your husband. Not that he is going to beat up everyone who talks to you, but that they wouldn't even dare because they respect him in his position, as you respect him in that position. If you don't respect your husband in the position of authority that he has, it will make him lose the fire that he has as your protector. Understand that you deserve the respect of your spouse as well as your peers, but your spouse must offer the utmost physical protection keeping you from harms way.

Personality Protection

"The LORD bless you, my daughter," he replied. "This kindness is greater than that which you showed earlier: You have not run after the younger men, whether rich or poor. And now my daughter, don't be afraid. I will do for you all you ask. All my fellow townsmen know that you are a woman of noble character." Ruth 3:10-11

From everything that he had learned and witnessed of Ruth, he saw that she was a virtuous woman. She was not a man chaser, she was not after any man for their money, and she kept herself until the time was come for her to be found. He protected her reputation by having her remove herself from that situation before anyone could see her. There is sometimes a point system with men, they would brag on how many women they have been with, how long it takes, and point fingers at to which women they had been talking about. Still today there is an unbalanced stigma connected to the relations of a man and a woman. Should a man be found in a relationship that is ungodly or unfaithful or even just beginning between two consenting adults, the man is said to be just. He is just being a man. He is held in high regard among his peers and even some women look at him as if they want to be the next notch on his belt. A woman, on the other hand, is looked at as being loose. If your mate is discussing your marital acts with someone else by saying what you are or are not doing in the marriage bed, he is not protecting your virtue and he is not protecting your character. No notes should be compared about what is and what is not going on in the bedroom. No discussions should be had about where you were or where you were not.

Husbands, love your wives, just as Christ loved the church and gave himself up for her to make her holy, cleansing her by the washing with water through the word, and to present her to himself as a radiant church, without stain or wrinkle or any other blemish, but holy and blameless. In this same way, husbands ought to love their wives as their own bodies. He who loves his wife loves himself. After all, no one ever hated his own body, but he feeds and cares for it, just as Christ does the church. Ephesians 5:25-29

He should be character building, not character breaking. He should be protecting how others look at you and how you look at yourself. Your character is interchangeable with your personality. What you think of yourself, how you carry yourself and how you present yourself in certain situations is carried in your personality. It is viewed by others as your character.

Boaz didn't want it to be known that she had been there. It was not common for a woman to go down to the threshing floor, but it was customary for a woman to show submission to a man in the manner she did to let him know her intentions. Without taking advantage of the situation, Boaz knew what his duties were and he was willing to accept them. Boaz was still a man of good standing. He was not only protecting her character, but he was also protecting his. By loving himself properly, he could love her properly. The bible tells us that no man has ever hated his own flesh, but because of some of the abuse and the discord that has been sown in the hearts and on the bodies of men, some will have to find a way to love themselves. It is really hard to care about someone else when you don't care for yourself. Destroying the bodies with drinking and drugs, or filling up the space of your skin with multiple tattoos to cover the pain and the scars of the past, it is hard for them to love you if they do not love themselves. Women are not the only ones with self-esteem problems. Just like you, they may have to transition and forgive and build and move to be able to love you the way that Christ loved the church. Do not accept anything less. He should be offering protection of your body as well as your personal character.

Provisional Protection

At mealtime Boaz said to her, "Come over here. Have some bread and dip it in the wine vinegar." When she sat down with the harvesters, he offered her some roasted grain. She ate all she wanted and had some left over. Ruth 2:14

It was custom, when you wanted to be hospitable to a stranger, you would offer them what was called "sop." It was a way of sharing a meal by eating from the same bowl, offering up the same thing that you are eating by letting them know that at that particular time, you were an equal with them and you would be welcoming them. Boaz did not have to sit and eat with his servants. He didn't even have to allow them a meal. As he did this, he showed Ruth that he was a humble man, and that he respected her for who she was and for what she had done in helping Naomi. This was Boaz first invitation with Ruth to share a meal. This was an opportunity to get to talk to Ruth and learn more about her personally. Some of us begin our dating lives over dinner, sharing a meal, being in a comfortable position and situation. Boaz even told his workers that as she went back out to work, to help her out. Pull out extra and leave them for her, and if she just so happens to go into the wrong area or does something wrong, don't embarrass her. He made sure she had enough to eat and he made sure she had enough work to be able to take home provisions for the family. When I was young, one of the things I remember my mother teaching me as a young lady beginning to date is that you don't allow a man to put his feet under your table if he hasn't brought anything to put on your table. It was the principle of the man bringing home the bacon, if the man brings it home, the woman will cook it. There were times when men were the sole providers for the home and even when they were just showing interest in a woman, men were expected not to show up at your door empty handed. Men were to show that they were offering some type of provision for the house hold. "*He gave me these six measures of barley", saying "Don't go back to your mother in law empty handed." Ruth 3:17*

Families today are made up of all kinds of units these days for a multiplicity of reasons. A lot of times it is not just a single person in a home anymore. When Boaz gave her extra, he was providing for her family. He did not want her to go home empty handed so he produced provisions for the family. If you have children and you are dating and eating steak and your children are eating Chinese noodles and hot dogs, how fair is that? I'm not suggesting you to take your children with you on your date, but make sure they are as taken care of as you. If your hair is done, their hair is combed too, if you are dressed to the nines, so are they. They are representatives of you, and if he cares about you and how you look, dress, and what you eat, he should equally be concerned about them. Should you be living in your mother's home but you are not tending to her care or the care of her home, shame on you. The condition of those surrounding you should be your immediate concern, and should he care for you, it would soon become his also.

Proper Placement

One day Naomi her mother in law said to her, "My daughter, should I not try to find a home for you, where you will be well provided for? Ruth 3:1

As a parent one of my main goals is to prepare my children for a good level of care once they should leave my home. Let me rephrase that, to prepare my children with a good level of care TO leave my home. The one thing that we attempt to do as parents is give our children a better life than we feel we had. We want to give them access to more things, expose them to more and even allow them more opportunities. When they reach a certain age and you have taught them certain things, you try to feel confident they will make great choices for their lives.

Naomi felt that Ruth had been with her long enough and she had taught her all that she needed to know, that she was prepared to leave the nest. She has been taught to work, she has been taught how to keep herself up and now it was time for her to be the woman that Naomi knew she could be. Naomi didn't just throw her out into the streets and allow her to fend for herself. She told her to let her help find a place that would be suitable and at least comparable to what she was accustomed to and she would be taken care of as well as she had been with her.

One of the things I have taught my oldest daughter is that in this day and age, I cannot choose your mate for you, but whatever man chooses you, be sure that he can care for you in the same manner as I have. Make sure before you leave home, he can give you the same quality of life that I have, that he can provide for you as well or even better than I have. When you send your daughters out on their own, you cannot choose their mates for them, but you can make sure that they are being treated as you would care for them or better. Their mate should be giving them the attention and affection needed as well as upholding them to others, building their characters, maintaining provisions and providing protection. Someone going upside their heads or treating them bad should not be allowed. You may only be able to speak to her and pray for her, but whatever you can do, make sure she is prepared to go. She may not like everything you say or even listen to the advice you give her at the time, but make sure you say it. She will hear it later. Give your daughters and sons every opportunity to have the best chance of a great relationship with themselves and others.

CHAPTER 5   It's all Relative

Am I what I want

"Who are you?" he asked. "I am your servant Ruth, "Spread the corner of your garment over me, since you are a kinsman-redeemer." Ruth 3:9

The aspect of independence and the individualism we have adopted as women, has forced us into an area of strength and solitude that has left us wondering about what we want, need and desire from a relationship. Let me break that down for some of you. We have gotten so strong and independent and adopted that mentality of I DON'T NEED NO MAN TO DO NOTHING FOR ME that we find ourselves, by ourselves and wondering why. We have set standards and prerequisites for our relationships with expectations that even we cannot live up to. Laying out rules to what we want, and need from a man, what we will and will not accept from a man, and what we just ain't gone take! We have stated that we are not going to settle for anything less than what we want, but we find ourselves stuck in what we get. What qualities do you have that will make a person want you? You have made this list of attributes, this job description and have laid out applications to a position that cannot be filled by anyone on this green earth.

When Boaz was startled awake by Ruth, she was unrecognizable to him. She had worked for him, she had shared a meal with him and even had a little conversation with him, yet he still didn't recognize her because something about her was different. Her reply to his question of who are you was as important as any other move of transition in her life. Her first words were "*I am.*" Ruth knew her identity. She didn't question him by saying, you know who I am, or don't you remember me. She didn't just reply by saying her name, she also stated her position, I am your servant. This was her position of submission. At this point she was letting him know, who she was and what she was about.

We want the position of wife, but we don't want to give up the position of authority. We are so strong, so independent and not in need of a man to do anything, that we push them out of their positions and wonder why they are not stepping up. If you feel there are certain things that a man should do in the relationship but you are telling him how to do it or challenging how he does it on his own with criticism or contempt, he will not stop trying. He may not do it the way you would have done it when you were on your own, but you are no longer on your own. Some of us choose mates based on their quantity and not their quality. We look at the muscles on the back and the accounts in the bank, not even considering the stability of the mind or the security of the man. Concerning ourselves more with how he looks, what he drives and where he works. How are you matching up with the mate of your search? We look at people and say I want a man with some money, but your accounts are in the red. I want someone tall with muscles and your gym membership card has dust on it. Can you be a good steward over money that can be comparable to your mate? You are looking for someone to be a good father to your kids from your previous relationships, but you don't want him to have any kids of his own. And if he does, you don't want to have any thing to do with them or the children's mother. Do you have a strong work ethic but he can't keep a job? What are your religious preferences? Are you both equally yoked? Do you both understand the positions you should hold in the family unit? Have you discussed the expectations of each position clearly? You cannot just assume someone knows what they are supposed to do. Are you in any way, shape or form what you want in a mate? Individualism is fine, but it has its place. You don't have to love all of the same things or even dislike all of the same things, but respect the position of the one that does.

Ruth and Boaz shared some of the same qualities and attributes. They were both respectful and respectable. They were both caring and cared about others. They both understood their positions and what they were willing to do to be together. Here is a little test to see for yourself how you compare to the mate you currently have, or the mate you are in search of. Being honest with yourself first will help you in the ability to be honest with your mate.

Qualities and attributes of a great mate

Qualities that I possess	Qualities that I desire to possess	Qualities that He possesses	Qualities that I desire for him to possess	How do our qualities match up?

In the first row, describe yourself by listing the qualities and attributes that you possess. Are you a great cook, God fearing, kind etc,...? In the next row, list the qualities you wish to possess. Do you want to be more giving, and maybe you desire to be more respectful or forgiving. The next two rows are about your husband or your mate, someone you may be considering marrying. What are his qualities and what are some of the qualities you wish for him to possess as your mate. Now, how do you all compare to one another? How well do you match up? If you have listed that you are a mother of five in your list but in his list you say, no children. How does that match up? If you list in his list that you want him strong, muscular and tall, but you are over weight, short and hate to exercise. How do you expect that to work? If you desire him to have financial security and you desire to learn to be a good steward over your money; that may be a good match for you. If you don't match up with the mate you are with, you may want to draw another line on the page and answer why it is that you have chosen to be with that person. Figure out what was the deciding factor which made you give up your true desires for a mate.

You may not find each and every quality you wish for a person. You may not even possess every quality that you think is important for you. This is where you have time for growth and discerning. We love to speak of not settling for someone or certain things in a person. Understand, every person you meet will have some sort of past. What can you deal with? When doing this challenge, don't only focus on the good. List some of the bad things also. You may find room for improvement in all areas. In the end you will notice your worth and the goodness that God created in you.

Clean Up

Wash and perfume yourself and put on your best clothes.
Ruth 3:3a

Naomi tells Ruth to get up, wash her self, perfume herself and put on her best clothes. When Naomi tells Ruth to get up and freshen up before she goes to present herself to Boaz, she is giving her vital information for her future. She is showing her how to properly present herself as a woman available for marriage. Naomi was showing her how to position herself to be found. Boaz has seen Ruth at work and she caught his eye, but she needed to prepare herself to be presented in a new way. She was not approaching him this time as a servant, but as a consideration to be his wife. Before you present yourself to the newness in life and the possibilities of moving forward you must prepare it. I have always thought that if you could catch a suitable mate's eye when you are not at your best, you could attract his heart when you are. Now trust me, I'm not saying that you should always walk around with your hair coiffed and a full face of make up, dressed to the nines and smelling like the perfume counter at Macy's. What I am saying is that there should be a difference between your appearance at home and your appearance outside of the home, if you are at work or play. If you were brought up in the 60's or 70's, then you were taught that there were different occasions for different styles of dress. You did not wear your school clothes outside to play and you didn't wear your church clothes out to a party. But today you will see people wearing the same outfit to church, school, parties and interviews. We have all seen it, or possibly done it ourselves. We've gone to the grocery store with rollers in your hair, wearing the pajamas you slept in last night, and scattering around in the fluffy pink house shoes you got for Mothers Day two years ago with pancake batter and juice stains on them. This is not the way a single woman, looking to be found by a mate should be walking around. It's not even the way a married woman should be walking around. We have all seen it, and probably done it. We take the kids to school or to the bus stop in the nice big fluffy robe and your hair still wrapped backwards in the scarf with the gel stains on it. You never know who will see you while you are out. Comb your hair, put on some clothes and then go outside. You may even say that you are not looking for anyone, but someone may be looking for you! The bible says "a man that finds a wife." But are you in a position to be found? When you are found, what are you looking like? You may not be interested in the man at the checkout line at the grocery store, but don't be fooled into thinking he is the only one at that store. There are many professional, single, God fearing men in the grocery store; there are the police or security officers, fire fighters, bankers, multiple delivery personnel from multiple companies, and many more. Don't underestimate the power of your exposure. Don't get stuck wearing your uniform and pulling your hair back into a pony tail all the time. Don't get comfortable walking around the house in your sweats with your head tied up.

By washing herself, she was getting rid of the filth and the grime of the day, she was purifying herself for the new task she was taking on and she was making herself fresh and making herself new. By putting on the perfume, it symbolized anointing herself. She was preparing her new body with oils used to protect, heal and to make her pleasant to be around. By putting on her best clothes, Ruth was removing the items normally worn by widows, now she was to portray herself as a single woman available for marriage. So as Ruth was washing herself, she was cleansing herself from everything that she had gotten all over her and collected upon her. As she was perfuming herself, she was healing the wounds from her past and protecting herself at the same time from new wounds. When she changed clothes she was removing the covering of the name widow and the disposition that came with it. Every time you prepare yourself to go into new territory, wash off the dirt and the collections of the day. Stand in the shower and watch the water wash the dust down the drain away from you. Purify yourself for your next task. When you put on perfume, allow the fragrance to flow through your system and begin to heal and protect your emotions while you also anoint yourself daily with words of encouragement. The right fragrance not only makes you smell good, but it can make you feel good also. Put on your best clothes. It is said when you look good, you feel good. Wearing clothing that fit your body type, clothes that you feel good in and the items that make you look the part you are trying to portray. Start your day looking and feeling good so you can get in the proper position.

Selfless Sacrifice

I have always been a giver, sometimes to a fault. I truly don't believe that I give to get anything in return. I was just brought up that way. If you see a need, do whatever it is within your power to take care of it. Throughout my lifetime, I have been on the receiving end of many levels of unselfish giving. People have helped feed and clothe my family. My finances have been blessed time and time again and many other types of personal blessings. In this past season of my life a couple of personal blessings in particular have stood out.

My husband and I took a road trip to support a family member with a group of friends. During the trip, my husband became very ill and the first night there had to be rushed to the hospital. It was discovered he had developed some type of poisoning in his system. When we reached the hospital he had a very low blood pressure and was looked at as a very sick man. As he spent four days in ICU away from home, my friends needed to return so they left us there in the care of their family. What started as a weekend trip, turned into a four day bedside vigil. We were in a new place, away from home, with new people that we had just met. We were strangers, but they treated us as their own family. *Hebrews 13:2 do not forget to entertain strangers, for by so doing some people have entertained angels without knowing it.* This family could have let us find our own way, but God allowed the unselfish acts of strangers touch our lives. They transported me back and forth to the hospital daily, fed me, gave me a place to sleep and once my husband was released from the hospital arranged transportation for us to get back home.

Ruth was a stranger, but the unselfish acts of Naomi and the unselfish acts of Boaz allowed her to experience the entertainment of angels. I often ask when others give unselfishly of themselves what is it that they are doing without? When someone is asked to unexpectedly give from their resources, not their surplus, but from their resources, they themselves must do without something. They may be taking from their bill money, their grocery money, or they may even be forgoing some type of personal item, but whatever it is, it is a sacrifice to be an unselfish giver.

Boaz was not the next in line to redeem the property of Naomi's dead husband. There was one in front of him (Ruth 3:12-13). Boaz was an unselfish giver, and he knew that the character of the brother before him was not. Even though Boaz knew these things, there were still certain allowances and respect that must be shown to him in order to do business the right way. As Boaz went to the city gates and gathered witnesses for the transaction, the brother who was the rightful next of kin came by. The law at the time stated that should a family member sell its property because of hardship and die before it could be re established, the next of kin or the kinsman redeemer should buy back the property in the deceased relative's name. Not only that, should he have left a widow, with no children, he should marry the widow, she comes along with the property, and the first born son will be named after the dead man to continue his name and give him a legacy.

The brother that was next in line he refused. He told Boaz, should I buy it, I may lose my own property (see Ruth 4:6). There was a chance that he would not have another son after the one who became heir to his brothers name, should that occur and he die, his name would not continue on. He was not willing to give up anything of himself, to help his brother. He was not willing to sacrifice what he had in order to gain more. It is a hard hand to receive when it is closed to giving. I am sure that you have worked really hard to gain what you have. You may have done it by the sweat of your brow or it may have even just been handed to you by your family, but the tighter you hold on to it, the greater the chance, that it will be all you have. The bible tells us to give and it will be given to us, good measure, pressed down shaken together and running over. Giving is a reciprocal act, although you may not receive back from the person that you gave, God will make sure you receive. People appreciate people who appreciate other people. If your mate is not willing to sacrifice what he has to gain you, you may want to look again at him as your mate. You cannot be the only one giving in a relationship.

Redemption

<u>The women said to Naomi: Praise be to the LORD, who this day has not left you without a kinsman-redeemer. May he become famous throughout Israel! He will renew your life and sustain you in your old age. Ruth 4:14-15</u>

The same people who Naomi saw when she was coming into the city broken, despondent and sad, where the same people who saw her when she was being redeemed. That same Lord that Naomi said had gone out against her was the same Lord whose name was blessed at this moment of redemption. That same name that Naomi was considering bitter, was now being blessed because of her redemption. To be redeemed is to be bought back or to be freed from a debt. The selfless act that Boaz did, released Naomi from the weights and the looks, the stares and the names. It freed her from the scrutiny and the cloud that she was under because of her loss. She has now because of her redeemer, gained back what some thought was more than she had lost and she was at this time reaping the harvest of what she had sown into Ruth earlier. Redemption may not come like you expect it. It may come in a different package than you would have liked it to. But you have to be open to receive redemption when it comes.

Boaz didn't marry Naomi, but through the redemption of Ruth, Naomi was adopted into this family and reaped the benefits. Rightfully so, Boaz should have married Naomi instead of Ruth. He said he bought all that was of Naomi's husband which included what belonged to the sons. But she set Ruth up to receive the blessings, she understood that she would be a part of the blessing. Naomi originally didn't understand what was happening to her and she was angry, bitter and hurt, but she was willing to go ahead and move forward in her purpose. She had to realize that she was put on earth to be more than just a wife and mother. Naomi's purpose was to bring Ruth to meet Boaz.

Sometimes when we don't understand something that is happening to us, but we should try to understand that it may be happening for us. *<u>And we know that all things work together for good to them that love God, to them who are the called according to his purpose. Romans 8:28</u>* Again, all things whether good or bad, when it doesn't look good, even when it may not feel good, is working out for your good. You may not know why that person was taken from you. Maybe the season was complete, it was for your good. You may not know why you lost that job. There may be one that has better benefits, it was for your good. You may not understand why you lost your house. Maybe the note was going up. It was for your good. God may be working through you to work a miracle so that others can see his redemptive qualities. You cannot be redeemed of something if you never want to lose anything. *for he chose us in him before the creation of the world to be holy and blameless in his sight. In love he predestined us to be adopted as his sons through Jesus Christ, in accordance with his pleasure and will- to the praise of his glorious grace, which he has freely given us in the one he loves. Ephesians 1:4-6*

    Christ redeemed us by his blood and adopted us into his family so that we could receive the benefits, and membership has its privileges. Being a child of God you have the privilege of being protected by the blood, you have the privilege of being restored by his love, and you have the privilege of being renewed by his word. Those same people who said that you would never be anything will see that you have been redeemed by God. The same ones who talked about you and told you to your face that you will never make it will be looking at you from a distance with awe in their faces. Redemption is from God, he guides your paths and gives you the answers to any question you may have about your life. Your life was not a mistake. The things that happened to you were not a mishap, you are a member of Gods family and he cares for you and he will take care of you if you only trust him. He knew before Naomi what was going to become of her life and all that she would be. If you would notice, although she felt her life was bitter and she tried to change her name, no one ever called her Mara and soon her life again matched up with her name. She was pleasant with Ruth, and she was pleasant with Boaz. She received in return what she put out. Before you were born, God knew you, and in his love he knew he would accept you into his family and through his grace and his mercy he extended his hand to you. Changing your name will not change your destiny. What God has for you, it is for you. You just have to move forward with whatever he gives you. Sometimes it may seem like his hand is against you, but if you remember that whatever is going on, is for your good and for his purpose, you will be able to look at it a different way.

Conclusion Love

1 Corinthians 13:4-13

Love is a word that is used very loosely in our society today. There are a few different types of love and they are used in different ways. People love things, people love food, people love places, and people say that they love one another. The love we are discussing here is the most selfless act that I know. Don't get me wrong, you can love all of these things and all these people. Love is nothing but a deep affection for a person or a thing, but the definition of love states nothing of condition. This type of Love is unconditional for those who truly understand it. The greatest understanding of this love is the love that God had for us by giving his son to die for our sins.

When Jesus came he stated to his disciples *"Do not think that I have come to abolish the Law or the Prophets; I have not come to abolish them but to fulfill them" Matthew 5:17* and he did this by showing love through grace and mercy and teaching us how to love. *Jesus replied, "Love the Lord your God with all your heart and with all your soul and with all your mind. This is the first and greatest commandment. And the second is like it; Love your neighbor as yourself" Matthew 22:37-39* We can recite the other 10 commandments because we learned them long ago and sometimes we really try to live by them. Should we choose to adopt the latter two that Jesus taught, and remember them, those others won't be that hard to live by. If we love the Lord with all our hearts and our souls and our minds, would it really be hard to not put another god before him? Loving him the way we should, wouldn't be any trouble giving his name the praise and not praising our things as gods. Should we love him the way we are supposed, we would not think to misuse his name. In loving our neighbors as ourselves, we would not think to envy them. Being jealous of what they have, we would respect what they have and not try to steal from them or to kill. Honoring your parents comes from love no matter how you think they should have raised you or treated you. Honor the position they have and the fact that they did the best they could with the information they had to work with.

Through love, Naomi took Ruth under her wing and adopted her as her own. She treated her as a daughter, teaching her about God and other important things she needed to know to survive in a new world.

Through love Ruth dedicated herself to Naomi and respected her as an elder and as someone who had more experience which she could learn from.

Through love Ruth worked and cared for Naomi. Through love Boaz protected Ruth's character and her body.

Through love Boaz provided for Ruth and Naomi by giving up of himself and accepting them into his household.

True love is not tit for tat, it is not measured by how much you do, how much you give or how much you receive. If you truly love or are truly loved, there is no keeping score, and there are no pay backs. Love doesn't take a long time to give back for what it has received. Allow for the transition to take place and the growth to come. Because of the love which Naomi showed to Ruth and the love which Ruth showed to Boaz, the circle of love was completed by the redemption of this family.

Through love, you can find the redemption that you need also. Through love, you can mend broken relationships, through love you can find peace of mind, through love you can bring families back together, through love you can recommit yourself to your marriage, through love you can find new fellowships and friendships and through love you can come full circle with the one that loves you the most and can share with you in all these things and more, our Lord and Savior Jesus Christ.

Amen

LaVergne, TN USA
07 July 2010
188732LV00001B/5/P